Learning to Live with High Functioning Autism

of related interest

Pretending to be Normal
Living with Asperger's Syndrome
Liane Holliday Willey
Foreword by Tony Attwood
ISBN 1 85302 749 9

Asperger's Syndrome
A Guide for Parents and Professionals
Tony Attwood
ISBN 1 85302 557 1

**Finding Out about Asperger's Syndrome,
High Functioning Autism and PDD**
Gunilla Gerland
ISBN 1 85302 840 1

Autism: An Inside-Out Approach
An Innovative Look at the Mechanics of 'Autism'
and Its Developmental 'Cousins'
Donna Williams
ISBN 1 85302 387 6

Parents' Education as Autism Therapists
Applied Behaviour Analysis in Context
Edited by Mickey Keenan, Ken P. Kerr and Karola Dillenburger
Foreword by Professor Bobby Newman
ISBN 1 85302 778 2

Eating an Artichoke
A Mother's Perspective on Asperger's Syndrome
Echo Fling
Foreword by Tony Attwood
ISBN 1 85302 711 1

The Self-Help Guide for Special Kids and their Parents
Joan Matthews and James Williams
ISBN 1 85302 914 9

Learning to Live with High Functioning Autism

A Parent's Guide for Professionals

Mike Stanton

Jessica Kingsley Publishers
London and Philadelphia

First published in the United Kingdom in 2000 by
Jessica Kingsley Publishers Ltd,
116 Pentonville Road,
London N1 9JB,
England
and
325 Chestnut Street,
Philadelphia, PA 19106, USA.

www.jkp.com

Library of Congress Cataloging in Publication Data
A CIP catalog record for this book is available from the Library of Congress

British Library Cataloguing in Publication Data
A CIP catalogue record for this book is available from the British Library

ISBN 1 85302 915 7

Printed and Bound in Great Britain by
Athenaeum Press, Gateshead, Tyne and Wear

Contents

To Dee, Matthew and Katie, this is your book as much as it is mine. Thank you for sharing it with me.

Acknowledgements

To all the staff and pupils at George Hastwell School who have taught me so much about the autistic spectrum over the years and all the parents, siblings and people with autism in the Furness branch of the National Autistic Society who have been such an inspiration and a source of strength to me while writing this book, thank you.

Author's Note

I wrote this book for some very busy people, the parents and professionals responsible for the care and education of children with autism. So I have avoided cluttering the text with references and footnotes. It is direct and to the point.

And the first point is in the title, *Learning to Live with High Functioning Autism*. Many people with autism have additional difficulties and need care and attention throughout their lives. Others have the potential to rise above their disability and enjoy a productive and independent life. They are the subject of this book. I use the term 'high functioning autism' because it communicates the possibility for success while reminding us that our children still face the enormous difficulties that come with their autistic condition.

The second point is that it is a 'parent's guide'. This is not a dry, academic account. I am passionate about autism. I am partisan. I have a point of view which informs this book. People with autism get a raw deal because their disability is not immediately obvious and because it is hard to understand. I wrote this book partly to explain to people what it must be like to be autistic. I learned it the hard way. It was hard on my son to teach me as well. It is easier to read the book.

A lot of the information in this book was found on the Internet. I have included the URLs or web addresses of sites where I found the information. Some of these may have changed. The World Wide Web is very much a work in progress.

Much of the information from parents and people with autism also came via the Internet in response to my appeals for information in both public news groups and semi-private e-mail lists. I have changed or omitted names out of respect for the individual privacy of my respondents. But I have also listed some of these internet resources. If there is such a thing as an autistic community it is to be found in cyberspace.

The generosity of spirit and the level of expertise freely given in this wired community is truly awesome. I thank you all for accepting me, teaching me and making this book possible. I hope I have got it right. If not I know I can rely on many of you to tell me!

CHAPTER I

Introduction

Matthew was diagnosed with autism in August 1997. He was 12 years old and had not been to school since January of that year. We thought the diagnosis marked the end of our troubles. Now the local education authority (LEA) would have to make the proper provision for our son. We soon discovered that the proper provision either did not exist or else it was too expensive. Even if the LEA were minded to pay (which they were not) there was still a waiting list. We became locked into a confrontation in which neither side could win and Matthew could only lose.

At the time I felt frustration at trying to explain the obvious to professionals and administrators responsible for service provision. When it came to autism they sometimes just did not seem to 'get it.'

'Yes, I know I said he is diagnosed with Asperger syndrome and now I am saying that he is autistic. That is because Asperger syndrome is an autistic spectrum disorder. Not everyone with autism has Asperger syndrome. But everyone with Asperger syndrome is autistic.'

'Yes, his academic abilities are above average and he did well in all the psychometric tests. But he only achieves this level one-to-one with an adult. He cannot handle peer group pressure which is why he runs away and hides when he should be in class.' etc. etc.

I wondered if my frustration was anything like that of my own son who had to deal with the lack of consideration and understanding from others on top of the problems that directly arose from his autistic spectrum disorder. No wonder that people with autism are prone to tantrums and panic attacks!

A period of ill health gave me the time to collect my thoughts and reflect on the steep learning curve I had negotiated in recent years. I began to realize how difficult it must be for busy professionals without direct experience of autism to understand my or Matthew's point of view. At the same time there had been a marked increase in reported levels of autism. It is not yet clear whether or not this increase can be explained by increased awareness and improved diagnostic facilities. Paul Shattock (1999) discusses the alternative theory that environmental changes may be contributing to an increasing prevalence of autistic spectrum disorders. Whatever the final outcome of this debate we can expect to see an increasing number of parents seeking diagnosis and intervention from service providers whose knowledge of autism may be lacking or out of date.

Parents, on the other hand, have a unique insight into their own child and often acquire detailed knowledge and understanding of autistic spectrum disorders. At the same time we sometimes struggle to share that knowledge in the midst of adversarial battles over diagnoses, definitions and resource allocations. There are so many occasions when I believe I could have expressed myself more effectively had I been less emotionally involved at the time. I am encouraged to express myself now by my discussions with parents and people with autism from around the world. I have tried to balance my sadness and anger at reading so many similar tales with the strange satisfaction that comes from realising that it is not just me. There is a problem out there and by articulating it to a wider audience perhaps I can contribute to the solution.

This 'parent's guide' has a three-fold purpose. I hope that the knowledge and understanding derived from this parent's experience can help other parents to realize that lots of us have been there, done that and survived. I hope you can learn from my mistakes.

I have also tried to write 'a guide to parents' for professionals so that an understanding of us and our problems can be added to the growing body of knowledge about autism that informs the choices made for our children's welfare and education. We are often made to feel as if we are either part of the problem or else not part of the solution. We ought to be recognized as the most important resource that our children have.

I also like to think that I am learning to view the world through the 'Asperger Lens' (Cumine, Leach and Stevenson 1998). One of the most disabling aspects of autism is the impairment of social cognition. In any encounter most of us are aware of at least three viewpoints; our own, that of the person with whom we are socially engaged and that of the wider audience. This is sometimes referred to as the Theory of Mind. We are aware that other people can have their own point of view, different from our own and can make a leap of imagination to share in that viewpoint. For people with autism it is an achievement sometimes to learn that people do have alternative viewpoints and it is an immense achievement to accept that another person's viewpoint can have equal validity with their own.

All too often we neglect to reciprocate. It is so easy to fall into the trap which says that, because the person with autism has a partial grasp of social reality, their view is therefore invalid. For every one of us our grasp of social reality is flawed. But it remains our reality. So it is for the person with autism. Imagine the furore if guide dogs for the blind were trained to bite their owners when they made a mistake. Then consider the pressure that we put on people with autism to conform to our expectations, and compare this with the lack of effort we put into meeting their expectations and appreciating their point of view. If we expect them to make allowances for us in order to live more easily in our world, the least we can do is to acknowledge their reality and make allowances for them.

CHAPTER 2

A Parent's Tale

For my son high school was his downfall. We live in British Columbia, by the way. We didn't have a diagnosis on him...we had a series of diagnoses but not the bundle. He spent most of his elementary school years between the public and private schools.

Grade 7 (the last elementary year here) he was in a 'resource room' and had the best of all his school experiences. The teacher made a huge difference. She knew how to tap into his strengths, she was working on self-esteem. He was like a whole different kid. She really pushed to be allowed to keep him for just one more year. She knew, and I believe, she could have made a lot more progress with a second year. The system wouldn't let him stay because of his size and his age (he was two years older than most grade 7's).

In Junior High he was, again, in a resource room. But Junior High means changing classrooms and where we live going from one building to another. I was assured he would have a Teaching Aide in all classes. Well, he didn't. They provided him with a 'peer tutor' in math but by his own admission she did his work for him.

Other classes such as cooking and typing he was on his own. He had the same teacher for both of these classes and at the parent–teacher interviews all she did was complain because he didn't come into typing and sit down and do the pre-class exercises. Had anyone explained these to him? Nope. In cooking he wasn't that interested and she complained that he kept wandering out into the hall. He somehow managed to get through the year and, of course, because of his age they moved him up a grade.

In grade 9 things went from bad to worse. The resource room teacher changed three times in three months. The last of the teachers decided that he wasn't worth even sending to class so she had him sweeping halls and delivering mail. He didn't mind. He is a very willing worker... until the other kids asked him what he was being paid to sweep. Nothing. Then the teasing started again. By November he was suicidal. The school called us in and asked us to remove him from school. They had had two recent suicides at the school and didn't want another one.

The most positive thing that came out of this was a referral to Children's Hospital where we did get the Asperger's diagnosis. They sent a home school teacher a few times for the rest of the year, but he didn't learn much. He was out of school for two years because I didn't know what to do with him. I put him in horseback riding lessons so he would at least have something to do.

We moved communities and I was able to get him into a provincial program for kids with autism. This classroom is in a local high school. Problem there was he was so much higher functioning than the rest of the kids. The lower functioning kids bothered him. He knew that the other kids in the school would shun him because of the classroom he was in. Teens can be so very cruel.

There were a lot of work experiences but most of them were things like picking up garbage at the bird sanctuary. We requested a barn and all he got to do there was clean out stalls, which he was very good at, but he wanted to work with the horses too. At the local SPCA they walked the dogs but were not allowed to go out of sight of the building. It was very degrading for him, I believe. Now he has a 'high school completion certificate' because he stayed in school until age 18. It's not really worth the paper it's written on.

He is now on disability, sitting around doing nothing all day, gaining weight, no friends. Once a week we take him out to a barn where he works for the day including working with the horses and is paid in riding. Social Services has been unable to help us because he 'falls through the cracks'. They got us in contact with a Career

Counselling place that promised him a job stocking shelves at a local store. He was looking forward to it. Six months later and after volunteering at a vets office (again sweeping floors when he had been promised he would be working with the animals) they informed us he was 'too high a risk' to put into the job stocking shelves. Why? Because the vets office asked him if he would like to wash the windows and he said no. He doesn't know how. I'm sure he would have done it if he knew how. He is very co-operative at home. He does what is asked of him.

So that is my story, for what it's worth. We have just found out there is a good chance we will be moving to Ontario in the next year. This may not result in a job for him, but since we will be living in the city of Ottawa there will be a wider variety of interests for him so a chance that he may at least get out of the house more often independently. He is capable. He just hasn't been given the opportunity to live up to his potential.

Many parents will recognize their own experience in this account, sent to me by a parent in Canada. We can all identify with some if not all of its themes:

- inadequate or late diagnosis
- a difficult transition from primary to secondary school
- inadequate classroom support
- lack of autism awareness among teaching staff
- lack of continuity
- teasing and bullying leading to depression and long gaps in attendance
- poor employment opportunities and the prospect of a life time on welfare.

Similar correspondence from parents in the UK and USA indicates that this is a widespread problem and not limited to or caused by the peculiarities of a particular national education system.

Of course, not everyone will share in this tale of woe. Many young people with Asperger syndrome enjoy academic success and find careers suited to their talents. They are able to meet and overcome the problems that prove the downfall of others. The truly fortunate will find a life partner who understands them and may even become successful parents themselves. However it does seem to be the case that when things do go wrong for our children, they can go badly wrong. If this book contributes to a few more success stories it will have done its job.

CHAPTER 3

Understanding Autism

The nature of autism

The first thing to understand about autism is that it is a pervasive, developmental disorder. It does exercise a lasting influence on every aspect of a child's social, linguistic and cognitive development. It is an organic brain disorder and is probably genetic in origin. The tendency for autism to run in families has been well documented (Frith 1991). Eventually it may be possible to identify the genetic keys that predispose a person to autism. It is likely that there are also environmental factors that can trigger a genetic tendency, either in utero or in the early years before brain development is complete. Trevarthen *et al.* (1999) maintain that, 'In nearly every case of autism, where appropriate techniques are available, some abnormality in the brain can be found' (p.92).

To complicate matters further there are likely to be a number of different mechanisms whereby environmental factors can trigger events in the brain and for some of them timing may be critical. The inefficient disposal of toxins; metabolic disorders, fragile immune systems, allergic reactions – each has its advocates. Some may trigger the autism. Others may exacerbate existing symptoms. More research is needed to discriminate between causes and effects in the behaviour of people with the autism.

It is not a temporary psychological phenomenon. At one time psychotherapy was the intervention of choice. Autism was, or so the theory went, the result of bad parenting. The child was traumatised as a result of aloof parents. This 'refrigerator mother' theory has long since been discredited. It is now recognized that if the parents are aloof or otherwise odd it is probably because they share a genetic predisposition to autistic behaviour and it is by no means uncommon for a parent to be diagnosed consequent upon the identification of an autistic spectrum disorder in one of their children. But the memory lingers on and all too often the parent is made to feel responsible for their child's behaviour and the autism is regarded as an excuse.

Nor is it a learning difficulty that can be fixed. The hurdles that a person with autism faces are permanent. Therapies, drugs, counselling, special educational provision can all help the person with autism to manage these hurdles more effectively. They will not remove them. With time the person with autism may become an expert hurdler but in the race of life they will never get to run on the flat. I sometimes think that, especially with the more able people with autism, it is not so much our efforts to normalize their behaviour but rather their ability to learn to cope and make allowances for us that is the key to their success.

The range of autistic spectrum disorders

The second thing to understand is that it is a spectrum disorder. It presents as a wide range of behaviours, of varying severity. But the underlying neurological disorder is the same.

Autism encompasses such a wide range of abilities and disabilities that both parents and professionals are often confused. There are so many different labels and diagnostic criteria. Children at opposite ends of the spectrum may appear so different that it is sometimes hard to believe that they actually share the same disorder. And even if they do, what is the use of a label that covers such a diverse range of problems?

The differences are striking. Some are mute while others will talk at length on their favourite subject. There are those who were never toilet trained and even smear their faeces, and others who are obsessed with hygiene and cleanliness. A majority have some form of learning difficulty that would be serious enough to warrant intervention even if they were not autistic. Others are college professors, computer programmers or successful businessmen or women. The savant type is well known through films like 'Rainman' but the majority of people with autism do not discover a special talent at odds with the rest of their abilities.

The range of differences only serves to make the similarities more striking. All share in a triad of impairments affecting language, social interaction and imagination. Note the word 'impairment' from the outset. It is often stated that people with autism have *no* emotions or interest in other people; that they have *no* imagination. This leads to the stereotypical view of an autistic person living in a world of their own, uncommunicative and impervious to the needs of others.

I cannot stress too much that people with autism are open to the full range of human emotions, thoughts and dreams. They may struggle with certain aspects of life because of their impairments but it is as well to remember that their difficulties, however bizarre, are not alien to the human condition. Every feature of autism has a recognisable counterpart in neurologically typical behaviour. Martijn Dekker (1999) offers this explanation of the term 'neurologically typical' (NT):

> To avoid having to use the term 'normal' to describe people who are not autistic, people at Autism Network International have invented a new term for people without neurological conditions such as autism: NT, which means 'neurologically typical'.
>
> This term has found widespread use in the entire online autism community, including even parents of autistic children. The opposite term is AC, meaning 'autistics and cousins', or people with autism and related conditions.
>
> This terminology is analogous to similar words in other disability communities, and can in fact help shape a community.

Certain features of the human condition are stunted while others are overdeveloped in people with autism. They often struggle to comprehend the deception, cruelty and double standards that we, sadly, take for granted in our adaptation to society. We should temper our eagerness to help people with autism adapt to our world with an equal resolve to make the world more amenable to them. We should also remember that we have much to learn from people with autism. Their accounts of learning to live with autism have done much to take academic research forward. Matthew once said to me, 'My teachers think they know more about autism than me because they have been on a course. But I have been autistic all my life!'

Definitions and diagnoses

The varied nature of autism has led researchers to identify different syndromes within the spectrum. It can be difficult to place children in these different subgroups for two main reasons. In the first place autism is a developmental disorder. The way it shows itself changes as the child grows and develops. Therapeutic interventions contribute to change as well so that a child who may fit the criteria for Kanner's autism in early childhood may grow up to resemble someone of the Asperger type. Kanner's autism is used to describe the condition in children who present with all the classic features from an early age while Asperger syndrome is loosely applied to children whose autistic features are less obvious and who show greater signs of intelligence.

Kanner was the first to publish a paper describing autism in 1943. Asperger's paper from 1944 was largely ignored as he published in German from within the Third Reich. But he was no nazi. Today we may detect a tendency in his writing to paint too positive a picture of potential outcomes for people with autism. He used the phrase 'autistic intelligence' approvingly as an explanation for genius. Frith (1989) suggests that this 'must be seen in the light of his fervent belief in the powers of education.' It should also be seen in the light of his desire to save his patients from the gas chambers that awaited all deemed defective by the Nazi state.

Second, as soon as you establish a set of subgroups a child comes along who does not fit any of them, hence the label PDD-NOS or pervasive developmental disorder – not otherwise specified. There are so many anomalies on the autistic spectrum that they have their own subgroup. The term atypical autism is also employed by some clinicians.

These difficulties find their reflection in the inconsistencies between diagnostic criteria around the world. The influential American Psychiatric Association have their own criteria out-lined in DSM IV. There are subtle differences with the criteria of the World Health Organization to be found in ICD 10 and significant differences with the criteria for Asperger syndrome used by Swedish clinician and researcher, Christopher Gillberg. These diagnostic criteria are reprinted in most standard works. I can particularly recommend the discussion that accompanies them in the book by Tony Attwood (1998) which is fast becoming the standard work on Asperger syndrome.

So a child with a language delay who becomes verbal and makes good progress could get one of many diagnoses: Asperger syndrome, high functioning autism, atypical autism, PDD-NOS are the most common. If just the language impairment is picked up a speech and language therapist may diagnose semantic-pragmatic disorder in which the child struggles with everyday aspects of meaning and usage despite often scoring well in formal language assessments. Subsequent improvements in language could result in the child losing their diagnosis altogether; only to present as a pupil with emotional and behavioural difficulties (EBD) in later years.

For this reason, while recognising the importance of focus-ing on subgroups for the purposes of research, some clinicians like Lorna Wing, herself the parent of an autistic child, favour the concept of an overarching spectrum disorder in which the features in common are as important as the individual differences (Wing 1998). It is the case that people with autism tend towards either the Kanner model of low ability and limited language or the Asperger model of typical to high ability with diminished language impairment. There is research to try and determine whether there are in fact many types of autism (analogous with the different forms of diabetes) in which an underlying common deficit expresses itself in two or more quite distinct syndromes.

Whether or not this turns out to be the case it is patently obvious that in practical terms there is a split. Education has been historically organized to meet the normal range of needs and abilities within mainstream schools while hiving off special needs to remedial departments or special schools. Pupils who tend to approach the Kanner model are, by and large, to be found in the special schools or classes. Pupils who more closely approach the Asperger type are more commonly placed within the mainstream school environment.

Until we can approach diagnosis with greater precision it is important to remember that most diagnoses are descriptions and not explanations. They are answers to previously asked questions. Some clinicians with rigid thought patterns and an obsession with the literal meaning of words (sounds familiar?) perseverate on the idea that the answers in their diagnostic manuals are the only possible answers and fail to come to terms with the additional questions our children raise.

CHAPTER 4

Diagnosis

Difficulties with diagnosis

Although autism has a fairly clearly defined diagnostic profile in terms of observable behaviour and developmental history parents often have difficulties obtaining a diagnosis. In part this is down to lack of awareness among professionals. The hospital consultants who are called upon for diagnosis sometimes completed their training at a time when autism was not even included in diagnostic manuals or was classified under schizophrenia. Others may have a detailed knowledge of Kanner's autism but have a very sketchy picture of Asperger syndrome. Our own consultant psychiatrist happily owned up to her own doubts and uncertainties about diagnosis before referring Matthew on to a specialist diagnostic centre. But it is not always easy for professionals to admit to gaps in their knowledge or expertise, especially given the mystique of omniscience expected of them by patients and public alike.

It must also be the case that hospital consultants have little incentive to give a diagnosis if they cannot provide treatment. There are a growing number of therapeutic interventions that can help a range of problems related to diet, sound sensitivities, tactile defensiveness etc. along with co-morbid conditions such as obsessive compulsive disorder. Still, it is a sore point with many parents that, while diagnosis is deemed a medical matter, intervention is mainly educational.

Parents would welcome agreed medical protocols to test for possible adverse reactions to gluten and casein, to measure yeast infections and check for levels of toxins. We would like to know if our child has a weakness in their immune system which counsels caution in relation to the normally benign vaccination programmes that are common in Europe and North America. We want to know if a metabolic disorder is aggravating our children's autism by causing an imbalance in their levels of vitamins and trace elements. Should we be restricting access to certain foods or using dietary supplements to boost vitamin deficiencies? Research in all these areas continues. The results are not going to lead to a cure. But if questions like these can be answered when a child is presented for diagnosis, relatively simple and inexpensive medical or therapeutic interventions may alleviate a lot of unnecessary suffering. If we can deal with their food intolerance or metabolic disorder or over sensitivity to environmental factors then the child with autism is going to be more amenable to the educational interventions and therapies that are already available.

We look forward to the growth of multidisciplinary teams that can provide a total package of diagnosis and assessment as well as provision tailored to our children's needs. This requires co-operation between different agencies responsible for health, education and welfare provision and is no easy thing to arrange. In the UK for example there is not always a coincidence between the boundaries of the area health authority (AHA) and the local education authority. My own LEA covers more than one AHA while my local AHA serves parts of two different LEAs! Correspondents in the USA tell of a different problem. Entitlement is enshrined in federal law. But services vary from state to state and accessing these services often depends on the interpretation of your medical insurance policy.

A signpost not a label

There has been a great deal of debate in the UK about the ethics of labelling children. This goes back at least to the Warnock Report on Special Needs (DES 1978) and is reflected in phrases like 'Continuum of Need,' 'Every child is special' or 'People First.' As a practitioner in the field of special education this has influenced me. Terms that purport to describe educational needs like Severe Learning Difficulties (SLD) and Profound and Multiple Learning Difficulties (PMLD) should not be used to define the whole child. I always write 'the child with profound and multiple learning difficulties' in preference to the abbreviated 'child with PMLD,' which is only a step away from the adjectival 'PMLD child.'

This has led to some resistance to ascribing labels such as 'autistic' to children. Knowing someone is autistic does not necessarily give the teacher any idea about the child's educational needs. Indeed, there are so many misconceptions about autism in the mind of the public that it could be worse than useless. How is the teacher whose knowledge of autism is gleaned from movies such as 'Rainman' to cope with an autistic pupil who has no savant abilities and is an absolute duffer at Maths? If you are familiar with the architectural drawings of Steven Wiltshire what are you to make of the child with autism who cannot even hold a pencil to write her name?

In our case the LEA argued that they did not need a diagnosis in order to identify Matthew's special educational needs. This is an admirable position of principle in the general run of things. Such an authority is not going to be blinkered by medical diagnoses and will look beyond the label to identify the needs of the individual child.

Educational psychologists have moved away from labelling children to describing their needs. There is provision for language difficulties, reading problems, behavioural support and so forth, and children are assessed in order to allocate provision. If there is no 'autistic' provision what is the use of the label? And if learning support is available for all the component parts surely it is enough to identify these individual needs and meet them?

This is persuasive except that many people with autism also assert that to deny them the label is to deny a valid part of their identity. It is also well established that early identification and intervention offers the best hope of a positive outcome and the most effective forms of intervention are educational. While all children are different and there can be no wider range of differences than on the autistic spectrum it is also true that all children with autism will share to a greater or lesser extent the following features.

- resistance to change
- attachment to routine
- social naiveté
- rigidity of thought
- over literal interpretation of language
- the potential to become obsessive and elevate routines into essential rituals that must be followed to the last detail.

Knowing this and understanding that a child's social and linguistic difficulties have an organic connection is surely of great help when devising interventions to improve language and social behaviour.

Most children with Asperger syndrome are in mainstream classrooms. Because language is often not noticeably delayed they may not even be diagnosed until their social impairment triggers behavioural problems, often around the time of puberty. Or else they will have some special needs identified – Matthew was 'a child of average ability with severe difficulties using and understanding spoken language' when he was three. This changed to 'severe emotional and behavioural difficulties with moderate language difficulties' when he was ten. We were told that he was 'one of a kind' by one professional. Finally, he was diagnosed with autism when he was twelve.

Correspondence with a self-selecting group of parents and individuals with autism who use the Internet to visit autism related mailing lists and news groups suggest that this is a widespread experience. There is no reason to believe that those without Internet access fare any better.

Our experiences

Parents' fears are often dismissed and they are not taken seriously.

When he was four, I was told he was over indulged by parents. My son, now 23, was finally diagnosed with Asperger syndrome at the age of 20.

At the age of about 14 months, I became concerned because Eli was still not talking. The only words he said was mama, and do-do (doughnut). I questioned his paediatrician at the time who just blew me off and said, 'ah, I wouldn't worry about it. All children progress at different stages…' He was diagnosed as 'Stubborn.' (the doctor said he would talk when he was ready… well he's four and a half now… apparently he is still not ready or just extremely 'stubborn.'

Yesterday I spoke to a parent who said that she and her husband were also given a diagnosis. Many times in the beginning when we first notice the child having a problem they poo poo us. It was written in the kid's records. 'Hysterical Mother. Imagines something wrong with child.'

This is a potentially dangerous situation for the family, especially if the verdict shifts from 'imagines' to 'invents' to 'induces'. This is the latest twist to the old chestnut that we, the parents, are responsible for our children's autism. Only this time we are alleged to be doing it on purpose. It is a real issue for parents whose children are high functioning and do not present with any major difficulties in the early years. Because children with high functioning autism often perfect a public persona which crumbles in the safety of their home environment it is often only the parents who witness their autistic behaviour. If we persist in seeking assistance for children who place all their efforts into appearing normal to the outside world we are sometimes not only disbelieved but may also be accused of deliberately fabricating our child's symptoms when they emerge. There is a serious mental disorder known as Munchausen's Syndrome by Proxy in which parents deliberately make their children appear ill in order to attract sympathy to themselves. Some parents of children with autism have found themselves accused of having this syndrome. This whole issue will be discussed in greater detail in the next chapter.

Then there are the arguments reminiscent of the old debate about dyslexia. Is it real or just a 'middle class' syndrome? For many years there was an argument about why apparently bright children struggled at school. Parents from middle class backgrounds refused to be fobbed off. They wanted to know what was wrong. Critics responded that there was nothing wrong. They just could not cope with having a low achiever in the family. The fact that initially there were a disproportionate number of middle class children with dyslexia lent a veneer of truth to this position.

As one parent wrote:

> The only one that really made us angry was the local authority Educational Psychologist who told us there was nothing wrong with her except that she wasn't very bright and we were middle class parents who couldn't cope with having a low-achieving child! She has just finished a BTech in Art and Design at Chelsea College of Art.

The reality is somewhat different. Low achievement and social and personal difficulties are almost expected of disadvantaged communities who are viewed as victims of their environment.

The search for a cause is more likely to be pursued if the subjects are rich or cultured. But that does not mean the overall incidence is greater among the middle classes. Working class people are just more likely to be misdiagnosed or not diagnosed at all. They can be caught in a disability trap along the lines of 'We were so poor we couldn't afford autism in our family. We were just thick.'

It can be difficult to get an accurate diagnosis.

> *There seems to be something but we're not sure what began at age eight and it was officially HFA/Asperger's at eighteen and a half (she is now 20). In between it was:*
>
> *'A reaction to hearing loss' (she did also have glue ear).*
>
> *'A difficulty with high level language processing.'*
>
> *'Some kind of dysphasia.'*
>
> *and finally,*
>
> *'Probably borderline Asperger syndrome but I won't put it in writing because the LEA will send her to an unsuitable school.'*

Even children with all the classic symptoms of autism can be misdiagnosed.

> *He is now 15 and has just got emerging speech. He appears on the Open University Psychology series as the boy rocking backwards and forwards to Postman Pat. The film features him as a classic Kanner type child.*
>
> *When he was three and a half a major London Hospital concluded: 'His mother recognises that he well (sic) behind in his development, possibly down to 18 months level of age. Even this is, I am afraid, a little optimistic since there is virtually a complete absence of any skills other than those which might simply be sensori-motor. As far as his interpersonal development is concerned, he is more like a child of nine months with strong mother*

attachment and well developed stranger awareness. There was no evidence of any autistic features during the time he was with us.'

Well he did have to be dragged on the train to London and by public transport to a noisy crowded clinic. No wonder he had strong mother attachment!

Sometimes there is a confusion of labels.

Atypical autism, obsessive compulsive disorder, autistic tendencies, and social and communication disorder seem to be the 'hip' diagnoses being dished out in our area at the moment. I know of one young lad who is labelled with 'atypical autism with semantic pragmatic disorder, language delay, global developmental delay and dyspraxia.' Won't tell you of the provision and placement offered to this child by the LEA though, as that is more frightening than the label!!

The first psychologist I took him to wrote down a diagnosis as this, taken from the DSM IV:

> *'Mixed receptive-expressive language disorder*
>
> *Phonological Disorder*
>
> *Learning Disorder*
>
> *OS (word retrieval; phonological processing deficit)*
>
> *Pervasive Developmental Disorder NOS'*

This was one diagnosis. Confused the hell out of me.

The second diagnosis… 'Severely dysphasic with secondary anxiety and some compulsive characteristics, not autistic or PDD'.

Third diagnosis… 'autism'.

Fourth by the same people as the third … 'PDD/NOS mild'.

If we accept that diagnosis is a beginning, a signpost that directs us and our children towards appropriate provision it is plain why so many of us go to great lengths to get the correct signpost. In its absence the child will still be labelled but it may be the wrong label and point in the wrong direction. There have been cases where adults were misdiagnosed as mentally ill when in fact they were autistic. While that is less likely today the experiences I have quoted suggest that many parents and young people with autism experience a catalogue of misdiagnoses, sometimes tragic, sometimes comic, but always frustrating.

This confusion delays appropriate intervention and makes it harder for parents to come to terms with the diagnosis and its consequences. Lorna Wing's (1998) book has a useful chapter on the problems faced by parents. We need time to get used to the news and deal with the range of emotions it can engender. According to Baron-Cohen and Bolton (1993) these can include a feeling of grief akin to bereavement, denial, anger and guilt. Failure to acknowledge these emotions can store up psychological problems for the future, lead to marital difficulties and affect relationships with other children within the family.

What is not always understood is that the young person with autism is also prone to these feelings. And with characteristic honesty they are not averse to sharing them. Guilt and remorse for a 'lost' or 'wasted' childhood; blaming your parents and punishing them for having you; inchoate rage against a world that is so tantalisingly close and yet denied. All these responses are possible and, typically, it is close family members who take the brunt of them. It is not all rage and anger though.

Perhaps the most poignant moment for us was when Matthew said, 'I am sorry. I wish I could have been the little boy you never had.'

CHAPTER 5

Conflict and Partnership

Parents want a diagnosis precisely because we believe that it will point the way to appropriate services. Only when we have struggled to obtain that diagnosis do we discover that the services are in short supply. We are particularly vulnerable at this time.

Local support groups, telephone help lines and the Internet have all provided self-help, counselling and guidance for parents of children with autism and for young people with autism themselves. Sibling groups have proved invaluable for brothers and sisters who have to come to terms with a disability that confuses many adults and then explain it to their friends.

If you are fortunate enough to live near one of the major diagnostic centres attached to a university they may provide back up to parents coming to terms with the diagnosis and offer lessons in parenting or a guide through the maze of welfare and educational laws that affect our children. Of immense value is the group work with siblings being done under the auspices of the Robert Ogden School, formerly Storm House School, which is part of the National Autistic Society and is based in South Yorkshire, England.

If this range of services were available to all it would probably be self-financing as the future demands on psychiatric and social services by distressed families decreased. Plus, the child with autism would receive an earlier, more positive intervention, improving their prognosis and reducing further the liability for long-term expenditure on care and education.

No two people respond in exactly the same way but many parents experience similar emotions. Sometimes we get stuck in a particular groove. Two distinct tendencies are the *Worrier* and the *Warrior*.

Parental responses – the worrier

The worrier parent cannot get over their guilt. They want to know why their child is autistic. Was it their fault? Is there a cure or therapy that can help their child that they are not trying? Whenever the media trumpets another 'breakthrough' in the treatment of autism it adds to the pressure.

They come across the wealth of anecdotal evidence that diets, vitamins and different drugs can help some children with some aspects of their condition. Of course, friends and relatives are always hearing about miracle cures and interventions. These are usually very expensive and only obtainable on the other side of the globe. So, why aren't you mortgaging your other children's college fund and your pension to cure your child? Don't you love him enough? Or perhaps he is not really that autistic? Grrrr!

If you are the parent of a child with severe eating or sleeping problems, destructive or self-injurious behaviours, tantrums or prolonged periods of distress, and you are getting little or no professional support or advice that actually works for your child then you will try anything. Without serious research into the worthwhile interventions they have to bid for credibility alongside the shysters and hucksters promoting their snake oil remedies.

The National Autistic Society has published a booklet which describes over 40 different approaches; some are dietary, medical or educational and some are just plain weird. Most are worthy of attention (NAS 1997). But there are very few people 'on the ground' to whom parents can turn for guidance. In the UK parents who approach their local health providers for 'alternative' therapies are often viewed as cranks. In the USA these treatments are more widely available *if* your health insurance is prepared to pay. So the worried parent has to face the prospect of confronting an unsympathetic medical establishment or living with the guilt that they are not doing enough for their child. This sort of dilemma can lead to passivity, resentment and bitterness directed at more assertive parents who should be your natural allies, thus increasing your isolation.

Parental responses – the warrior

The warrior represents the other side of the coin. They are going to get the best there is for their autistic child. They have their rights and if something is not done someone is going to pay. There is nothing wrong with trying to get the best there is for your child so long as you do not lose your way. My own trajectory from worrier to warrior was fuelled by guilt at not being assertive enough and then overcompensating by taking up a completely adversarial position. With hindsight it sometimes appears that I was less concerned with what was right for my son than I was with the desire to get the faceless bureaucrat whom I blamed for all our grief.

Breakdown and conflict

It is easy to see how this can happen. The parents notice something about their child. Their fears are dismissed. They read an article about autism and recognize their child in the article. They research the subject. They pester the authorities. They become a problem to be dealt with while the child's needs are ignored.

This is a direct result of ignorance on the part of professionals. They do not understand that a child with Asperger syndrome may not present with any difficulties at school or home for a long time. This is because in the fairly stable world of childhood it is possible for a bright kid with autism to work out rules of conduct and live by them. Young children can be notoriously rule bound with a strong sense of right and wrong based on rigid application of the law. This fits well with autism. A lot of schooling is about the acquisition of knowledge. Diligent work habits and a good memory for facts, along with an interest in adults and precocious language skills are again a common feature of some, but not all children with autism. If a child with Asperger syndrome has the above features and does not have any obvious motor or sensory issues they could pass unnoticed for quite a while.

But the demands of the system change as they get older. The emphasis shifts from rote learning and rule bound behaviour to questioning and understanding, making moral choices, rebellion, changing rules and changing dynamics within the peer group. Above all there are the psycho-sexual and hormonal changes to themselves, the growth spurts, the changes to their bodies and the unwanted thoughts and desires.

Another feature of autism is that children often maintain a fragile exterior calm in public to mask their inner turmoil. They may survive at school, appearing well behaved and getting good grades, only to experience meltdown at home, presenting all the problems that only parents see. One young man described to me how:

> Since I entered high school I've perfected my 'Outward appearance'. I appear to be a normal person, and I recognize any emotion (well, almost any) without thinking. I drive my mum crazy with my uncontrolled tempers and rudeness. It's hard to keep this appearance all day, so I stop when I get home. I'm not really fun to be with when my 'social mode' is switched off, but I turn it on whenever anyone except my mom gets close. I guess my mom's the only one (except for me, then) who suffers from my Asperger syndrome.

Hence you get a teenager with bizarre behaviours at home. Parents are at their wits' end. School either says there is no problem or else identifies a sudden and inexplicable change in school behaviour. In a structured test environment with the psychologist, one-to-one and no distractions or peer group pressure the pupil shines.

So what is the diagnosis? 'Must be autism' – or – 'I blame the parents'.

Too often it is the latter when it should be the former. Some parents have found themselves placed in a very invidious situation. In the course of battling with the authorities many of us would probably score highly on a profile like this one (my comments are in brackets)

- Are often upper class, well-educated persons (*articulate, educated parents are often the best at obtaining services from a system that is not too user friendly*).

- Remain uncharacteristically calm in view of the victim's perplexing medical symptoms (*we all know that stress makes our children worse*).

- Welcome medical tests that are painful to the child (*only if they are necessary*).

- Praise medical staffs excessively (*only the good ones that understand autism!*).

- Appear to be very knowledgeable about the victim's illness (*we have to be knowledgeable about our children as not too many other people are*).

- Have some medical education, either formal or through self-initiated study or experience (*I have had to teach myself some basic medical stuff in order to evaluate conflicting theories and therapies for autism*).

- Might have a history of the same illness as the victim (*there is a genetic element to autism*).

- Typically shelter victim from outside activities, such as school or play with other children (*I have withdrawn my son from school to protect his mental health. Many parents become home educators because the schools cannot cope with their children*).

- Allow only selected persons close to their children (*yes, the autism friendly ones*).

- Maintain a high degree of attentiveness to the victim (*some people with autism benefit from 24-hour provision, seven days a week. Most of us are papering over the cracks in available provision*).

- Seem to find emotional satisfaction when the child is hospitalized, because of the staff's praise of their apparent ability to be a superior caregiver (*so, we respond well when professionals praise our parenting ability? There's a novelty!*).

Unfortunately this list is taken from a profile of Munchausen Syndrome by Proxy offenders drawn up by the FBI! (Artingstall 1995)

Munchausen Syndrome by Proxy (MSBP) is a serious condition in which a caregiver, often the mother, invents or even induces symptoms in their child in order to secure medical treatment that may result in physical or psychological harm or even death. This is a form of child abuse and, while the causes are not always clear, the perpetrators are clearly the victims of their own mental disturbance and probably derive some satisfaction from the attention and sympathy that accrues to them as carers of the 'sick' child. They often choose their victims carefully.

> The abuser will look for potential victims who cannot communicate and therefore cannot deny the symptoms or complain about deliberate attempts to induce the symptoms. Alternatively the victim may be a child who is willing to collude with the abuser by entering into the pretence of some medical disability. Accordingly, those young children with developmental disorders like autism may well be ideal victims for abuse of this kind. (Connor 1999)

This is very important. Impairments in communication and social understanding make all children with autism vulnerable to abuse. The abuse scandals that emerge concerning special schools and care facilities conform with the trend for potential abusers to seek employment that gives them access to vulnerable children. It is every parent's nightmare that their child might be abused and be unable to report it. But it does not follow that because a child is more vulnerable to abuse his or her parents are more likely to be offenders.

It is a bitter irony for some that in seeking a diagnosis of autism for their child, a neurological condition recognized by the World Health Organization and the American Psychiatric Association, parents find themselves accused of a syndrome that has yet to be accepted by these influential bodies. Moreover, 'diagnosis' of MSBP is often made by nonmedical personnel such as police officers or social workers based on a parental profile that owes more to forensic psychology than to clinical practice. Instead of attending to the child's needs they surmise that the parent is the one with problems and interpret all the evidence of need as proof of the parent's condition.

Judith Gould drew attention to MSBP in the NAS magazine *Communication* (Gould 1998). While not minimizing the dreadful problem of MSBP or denying that there may be parents who make false claims about an alleged autistic condition, she is quite clear that the child needs to be referred in the first instance to a professional who understands autism. She concludes:

> If, at the end of a careful evaluation, it is concluded that the parent or other carer has invented or caused the child's seemingly autistic behaviour, the opinions of independent experts in the field should be sought. The implications for the family of a diagnosis of MSBP are so devastating that every care must be taken to avoid a mistake. It is not a light matter to be responsible for ruining the lives of a whole family.

A chilling confirmation of this occurs in the FBI profile referred to earlier, which states that 60 per cent of mothers accused of MSBP attempt suicide, including those who protest their innocence. The bulletin neglects to inform us how many of these attempts are successful.

Partnership

Both warriors and worriers can become overprotective towards their children. Because of this the children may learn to define themselves by their condition. One example might be the child with a learning disability who could manage to achieve a reasonable level of independence in adult life. But if given a sick role to play they may learn to play it to perfection and always be dependent on others for things they ought to be capable of themselves.

It is easy to see how this could happen. The parent is told their child has a problem but receives very little support in coping with the news. For some the child becomes their permanent baby that they will love and look after for ever and ever. Such parents are very loving but can impede a child's progress by doing everything for them and spoiling them completely.

These children have a genuine difficulty and parents who want what is best for them. The parents just need some guidance and reassurance. No professional is allowed to be alone in a room with children until they have completed their training. Parents of children with special needs are expected to get by on their own with no training. As primary caregivers we ought to feature prominently in the in-service training budget of every agency that deals with autism. Because if we cannot cope you are going to have to train someone else to replace us and pay them as well.

Often aspects of both warrior and worrier are present in the same person at the same time. We are used to living with contradictory ideas. It is only when the contradictions become too acute that breakdown occurs, and many parents do experience breakdowns.

So those dealing with parents need to be aware that we have special needs as well. Health and education officials ought to develop a 'bedside manner' and be gentle and supportive. Above all what we need is honesty. If the provision is not there because of cuts in government expenditure and the authority cannot afford what is best for my son, tell me! Do not pretend that you can meet his needs within existing provision when it is patently obvious that you cannot.

Parents do want a partnership with professional agencies to help our children. If the system needs a shake up we can do the shaking. We are not constrained by professional etiquette. We can court publicity in ways that might be inappropriate for public servants and state employees. Both worrier and warrior can be positive if we worry about the things that matter and go to war against the right targets. We can be your friends in low places, humbling the mighty.

So, to all who have dealings with the children with autism I make this appeal.

Take the parents into your confidence, as we take you into ours by entrusting you with our children's future. Do not patronise us, dismiss us or attempt to pigeonhole us. We may not always know what is best for our children. But, rest assured, we always want what is best for them.

CHAPTER 6

Brothers and Sisters

It is not easy for the other children in a household when a family member has autism. The person with autism is constantly trying to make sense of a world that seems to lack coherence but ought to have it. They will impose order where none exists. Accidents do not happen. That is too terrifying a prospect. They are caused and someone must be to blame. Unfortunately, childhood is very accident prone and it is usually the sibling who is nearest to hand and most likely to get the blame. Katie, Matthew's sister has many memories of the problems.

> *One time my brother and I were playing 'Thomas the Tank Engine.' I was a toddler at the time. Matthew was four. We had a toy Thomas with wheels. It was big enough to sit on. While Matthew was sitting on 'Thomas' it broke under his weight. Of course, the whole thing had to be my fault, even though I was halfway down the path waiting for my turn at the time.*

Being blamed, resenting it, feeling guilty because he is autistic and cannot help it. Siblings have a lot to put up with. Often expectations of them are higher and sympathy is less because they are not autistic. Matthew's sister has this to say.

> *Being a parent/guardian of an autistic child is hard. Being a friend or a sibling or both is also hard. Oh, and being autistic is hard too. But no matter which of the above groups you fit into someone is always there to tell you, 'He's the one with problems. What have you got to complain about? Don't pity yourself. It is worse for your Mum/Dad/Sister/Brother etc.'*

What the person who is saying this does not realize is that even IF your problems are smaller than someone else's it does not mean they are small. They still count and there is no way they are going to go away until you tell someone. If you talk to someone who you can trust, then they can offer a fresh point of view and some solutions. Sometimes talking to someone from outside the family who won't or has not already taken sides is easier.

The pressures on siblings should never be under estimated. They may be on the receiving end of violent tantrum behaviour or their property and privacy may be constantly interfered with. Younger ones, particularly, can have a very hard time at school if they have to follow an Asperger relative who has acquired a reputation for bizarre or extreme behaviour. My own daughter's choice of secondary school was severely limited by her quite understandable desire to go to a school where she would not be known as 'the nutter's sister'. Even so she is known in our area as his sister and hence is regarded as fair game by some of the more mindless yobs and bullies who rejoice in their own so-called 'normality'.

One benefit of being the younger sibling of a child with autism is that you do not know any better. Growing up with an older brother or sister with autism 'is' normal. Weird rituals, permanently stressed out parents, sleepless nights; isn't that everybody's experience? The older siblings of a child with autism often remember what it was like to enjoy a normal family life and resent the loss.

But for all siblings the burden is great. Too often the system is not sympathetic to their needs. What is the point of diagnosing emotional and behavioural difficulties in a disruptive teenager if you ignore the fact that he cannot remember the last time his sleep was not disturbed by the ritual behaviour of his autistic brother? This case was referred to at a recent conference, an annual event organized by Cumbria NAS and Cumbria LEA. Geoff Evans, from the Robert Ogden School, spoke at length about their work with siblings. The text is available on the Autism 99 web site and is a model of good practice (Evans 1999).

Closer to home Katie met up with a number of girls of similar age at a siblings group organized by the psychology department at our local hospital. When this particular project ended they continued their friendship with sleep overs, cinema trips and meetings at our house which usually involved pizza, cola and lots of mutual support and understanding.

I know that lots of parents try to organize play dates for their child with autism. If you are in a local group the chances are that you will find a number of siblings who would also welcome the chance to come together. Having friends who will not be put off by the social naiveté of your brother because they have one just like him at home can be a tremendous boon.

CHAPTER 7

Early Years

There are at least two easily definable paths of development for children with Asperger syndrome or high functioning autism. There are those who present with all the symptoms of classic autistic in infancy and improve with time. The impact of their autism may lessen as they learn to cope with it. Then there are those children who may pass unnoticed during the early years. The impact of their autism increases with age as subtle but fundamental differences take on significance as the child develops and matures. Of course, there are many variations on these archetypes as well.

Miracle cures

The first type are sometimes used as examples for some of the alleged miracle cures for autism that make headlines for a while and then disappear. What usually happens is that a child who was very hard to reach suddenly begins to talk, or make eye contact or use the toilet or stop harming themselves. The parents cast around for an explanation; a drug or herbal remedy perhaps. Other parents try it and some have similar success. Secretin is just the latest in a long line of these so-called cures. Sometimes they are really onto something and have discovered a means to alleviate some of the more debilitating symptoms. The Allergy Induced Autism group is a case in point (Kessick 1999). Sometimes it would have happened anyway. Autism may result in disordered development but development still happens. It is also true that early identification and intervention reap the most handsome rewards both in terms of quality of life for the person with autism and reduced demands on service providers in the long term. But often a quite subtle mechanism is at work.

Children with autism typically inhabit a world of chaos, our world. Their impaired ability to share in our common sense interpretation of experience leads them to impose their own uncommon sense of order and meaning. This can lead them to act in ways that are quite at odds with our ideas of appropriate behaviour. So we cajole, threaten, plead and generally respond in ways that add to their confusion and confirm them in their own version of reality. We seem quite mad and not to be trusted.

Then their autism is recognized and we change. We follow more consistent programmes of behaviour management. We stop punishing them for non-compliance. We lose our sense of powerlessness and frustration. We think we know what is going on now and are calmer and more predictable. We may start them on a course of medication or a special diet or we may visit a therapist. We begin to lose our own guilt and anger and no longer project them subconsciously onto our offspring. And they improve. Surprise! Surprise! They may still be autistic but their autism is no longer so disabling and we are able to enjoy our children and teach them to enjoy us.

There is also the danger of regretting past mistakes and adding to your guilt. 'If only I'd known... I wish I hadn't done that...' etc. etc. You have to forgive yourself. You did the best you knew and when you learned better you did better. Nobody can expect more than that.

And let us remember for every 'cure' that makes the headlines there are many for whom progress is slow and undramatic. Parents and children work hard for every little gain and for some these gains are heartbreakingly few. We should also remember that at this stage it is often impossible to tell who will turn out to become both a PhD and successful businesswoman, as happened to Temple Grandin, and who will continue to need care and attention 24 hours a day, seven days a week for the rest of their lives.

Identification of children in this category ought to be more straightforward now that autism is joining the mainstream of readily diagnosed childhood complaints. Parents and profess-ionals just have to remember that when intervention brings visible improvements, however dramatic, it does not necessarily mean that hidden causes have been eliminated. The intelligent child with autism who learns how to be normal on purpose is still a child with autism. Imagine how devastating it can be if you keep your side of the bargain, do your utmost to conform and then, just when you need it most, support is withdrawn because your behaviour suggests that you have been 'cured'.

Missing diagnoses

The undiagnosed or misdiagnosed are far more likely to be those children who present as 'normal'. Maybe they have specific difficulties that are identified or are seen as gifted while their overarching spectrum disorder is missed. My earlier discussion of MSBP focused on some of the harmful consequences for parents of late or misdiagnosis. The consequences for children whose autism is not recognized can be tragic in other ways. I still wonder what if... What if Matthew's condition had been identified earlier? What if we had responded correctly to his fears and obsessions? What if we had withdrawn him from school earlier? Would he have grown up with OCD, a victim of bullies and driven to school phobia? Whatever, I have no doubt that his passage through childhood would have been easier. And, despite what I wrote earlier, forgiving yourself is easier said than done.

A young woman who was regarded as gifted but odd during childhood, described to me how pretending to be normal actually led to her denying her own identity and personality. She could fool her peers and her teachers for a while but she could not fool herself. She suffered a severe identity crisis in adolescence and collected a raft of inappropriate psychiatric diagnoses and treatments before meeting a psychologist who understood autism and helped her to discover the path back to her own identity.

Early intervention

How can we identify these children sooner rather than later? Reading Matthew's early reports with the benefit of hindsight certain features leap out.

- Do they look when you point things out?
- Do they seek adult mediation in dealing with their peers?
- Do they take you by the hand and lead you instead of pointing to things that they want?
- Do they 'hover' instead of participating in play with other children?
- Does their toy play seem to lack the spontaneity and exuberance of other children?
- Does speech lack expression or show erratic variations in tone or volume?
- Do their conversations tend to be monologues in which they are overly serious?

This is by no means an exhaustive diagnostic checklist. But if we had been alert to the possibility of autism as an explanation for Matthew's difficulties we might have given these factors equal weight with the more insistent evidence of ear infections and hearing difficulties.

There is sometimes a strangeness, not necessarily enough to cause alarm or even to alert the parents, especially if it is their first child. But an outsider (perhaps a health visitor or play group leader) may notice something; not enough to invoke procedure but sufficient to say, 'Watch this child'.

One problem we all face then is what to say. This is especially acute for us when we see echoes of our own child in another yet the parent seems blissfully unaware that anything is wrong. Broaching the issue too early, when the parent is not ready for the news may lead to denial and a loss of trust and friendship between us. Leaving it too late means valuable time is lost. And, what if we are wrong?

Matthew dealt with that problem in his own way when he approached a complete stranger in a playground in the Lake District and asked her, 'Has your son got his diagnosis yet?' He recognized himself in the toddler and was giving the bemused mum chapter and verse on autism before we could intervene. Fortunately she was already aware that there were problems and we were able to help. Matthew's manner and behaviour gave her encouragement regarding her own son's future.

A less haphazard approach than Matthew's is offered by initiatives such as the Early Bird Project and the CHecklist for Autism in Toddlers (CHAT). CHAT is currently being developed for use by family doctors and health visitors. It is not a diagnostic tool as such but an early warning system to alert professionals to the possibility of autism in children as young as 18 months. It is

> a short questionnaire which is filled out by the parents and a primary health care worker at the 18 month developmental check up. It aims to identify children who are at risk for social-communication disorders. It consists of two sections: the first nine items are questions asked to the parents, and the last five items are observations made by the primary health care worker. The key items look at behaviours which, if absent at 18 months, put a child at risk for a social-communication disorder. These behaviours are (a) joint attention, including pointing to show and gaze-monitoring (e.g. looking to where

a parent is pointing), and (b) pretend play (e.g. pretending to pour tea from a toy teapot).

The above is taken from Sally Wheelwright's contribution to the NAS web site. Her address is in the resource section.

Early Bird is an intervention project for pre-school children with a diagnosis on the autistic spectrum. Its purpose is to teach parents and professionals ways to develop play and communication skills in pre-school children with autism. Professionals who work with children with autism undergo training to become licenced practioners who go into the family home and work with families who have a child with autism. They assess the child's needs and train parents to understand and work with their own child.

Early Bird began as a local initiative developed by the NAS in South Yorkshire. It drew on the work of the Hanen Programme of early intervention which helps children with developmental difficulties to communicate via a focus on family activities. The original Hanen programme, developed in Canada, was unsuitable for children with autism because it did not take account of their specific difficulties with communication. According to a report in *Communication* (Network News 1999) the latest programme from the Hanen Centre, 'More than Words' has been designed for children with autistic spectrum disorders. Instead of working in the home it brings small groups of parents together for training courses of about three months duration, roughly the same as the Early Bird Project. Parents practise the techniques they have learned in the home and the sessions are videotaped for individual feedback with their tutor.

Another popular early intervention programme is the system of Applied Behavioural Analysis (ABA) that was pioneered by Professor Lovaas in the USA (Lovaas 1980). It is very intensive and expensive to implement in all its thoroughness. Properly implemented this is another useful technique that works for some but not all children with autism. The parent has to employ an ABA therapist and usually recruits a team of volunteers to help with the programme of carefully planned activities that can take up to forty hours a week. Contact addresses for ABA, Early Bird and the Hanen Centre are all listed in resources.

Then there are child centred programmes such as the Stanley Greenspan's Floor time (Greenspan, Weider and Simon 1998) and Intensive Interaction, a similarly humanistic approach developed in the UK by practitioners disillusioned with the effects of behaviour modification in institutional settings in the UK (Nind and Hewitt 1996). These are not autism specific but I like their philosophy that behaviour is not a problem to be dealt with. Instead it is seen as a purposeful activity. It is our job to understand the purpose, enter into the world of the child and teach more effective means of fulfilling that purpose.

It is difficult to compare all these methods because they are based on competing psychological or philosophical approaches. If one method works for your child what is to say that any of the other approaches would not work as well? But if it does work for you and your child what parent is going to stop and try another programme in the interests of scientific research? All of them work with enough children to make them worthy of attention. Parents have to check out what is available in their area and decide if they are comfortable with it. No matter how many people it has helped; no matter how impeccable the research findings or the credentials of the therapist; if your instincts say 'No' then an approach is probably not for you. Even if you go ahead it probably will not work because you will be half-hearted in your implementation.

On the other hand, if an approach commands your con-fidence and makes you feel empowered you will apply it consistently. You will not be interested in the minutiae of academic debates about its validity just so long as it works for your child. There is an important lesson here for service pro-viders. It is inevitable that within the remit of a specific fund-holder one or two approaches will tend to dominate. The temptation is always there to squeeze the child to fit the available provision even if it is not entirely suitable. But children with autism are very particular about the way they are squeezed and if an approach is not working for a child you have to change the approach whatever the short term financial costs or administrative inconvenience. This is an even more important issue for parents of school age children.

CHAPTER 8

Childhood

Once you are past the anarchy of the toddler years children can be quite rule bound creatures. They tend not to go in for introspection, abstraction and complicated hidden feelings. What you see is what you get. The child with high functioning autism, by careful observation and judicious use of logic and intellect can divine the unwritten laws of childhood, and while they may not always understand they get quite good at predicting what their peers are going to do. Just as important, they can often work out correctly what their peers expect of them. In fact, the carefully handed down traditions of childhood, the rhymes and songs, the games and rituals are just what the child with autism relishes. OK, so they may be just a little more pedantic than their peers in enforcing the law but at this stage it seems only to be a question of degree.

This can be a golden time for parents and children with autism. The confusion of the early years is behind us. Adolescence is a long way off. At school, stable class groupings give you time to develop a circle of friends or at least of children who are sympathetic to your child's difficulties and supportive. They will help him develop social skills and build his self-esteem.

We can educate the school as well. My son's most common complaint is that we take his achievements for granted and always expect him to do better. It is a fair point. Our children need time to savour their success and may react badly if they think they are being pushed too hard. Some children with high functioning autism are very bright. But the teachers need to learn that just because they have done so well they should not always be expected to do even better. If you have just climbed a mountain you need time to enjoy the view. There is plenty of time to hang glide off the top later.

Even the most stable periods in a child's development contain the seeds of change. I do not fully accept Piaget's thesis that there is a distinct transformation in the way children think, in particular in the transition from concrete to abstract thought prior to adolescence. But I do accept that a time comes when we no longer think as a child and we do expect children to use their knowledge creatively and demonstrate a higher understanding as they get older (Donaldson 1978). This can cause problems for our children as they approach puberty.

Up until then they can usually get by on the basis of prodigious knowledge and memory. Their ability to talk at length and appear knowledgeable on a range of subjects often endears them to their primary school teachers. Classmates will tolerate their odd behaviour because they can be relied on always to know the right answer. They are bright, talkative, comfortable with adults. Teachers have high expectations of these 'little professors' so they are pushed to develop their understanding, to answer 'Why...?' and 'What if...?' This can come as something of a shock. Why do they have to think about reasons when they already know the facts? Facts have been their mainstay for years, fixed and reliable. Now the teacher wants their opinion. Instead of learning from her, she expects them to argue with her, to discuss!

At the same time they begin to realize that they are being left behind by a peer group who are experiencing rapid development in social skills. They are beginning 'to individuate themselves in the midst of society', as Aristotle observed. Children with high functioning autism, on the other hand, begin to individuate themselves outside of society. For the first time in their lives some of these gifted but odd children may have to face the fact that in important areas of ability they are not the best. As social skills increase in importance their deficiencies in this area are often cruelly exposed. A late developing theory of mind brings awareness that other people have different thoughts, different identities. With this comes the suspicion that perhaps they are the odd one out. They are the strangers who feel excluded without really understanding why.

CHAPTER 9

Adolescence

All people with autism have difficulty coping with change. You do not need a degree in psychology to work out the impact of adolescence with its constant changes on our children. There are three main areas of difficulty.

Peer group changes

All begins to change with puberty. Part of the psychological change of adolescence is that you question the rules, rebel against them, make up new ones. Instead of chasing the girls away the boys are chasing after the girls. They, in turn seem more willing to be caught, at least by some of the boys. The child with autism suspects that things have changed. He does not understand and so he asks why and breaks the unwritten rule that states that, 'Thou shalt not talk about the unwritten rules.' Rather like the time I asked the price of an item in an upmarket shop and was told, 'If you have to ask the price you cannot afford it,' our children are told that if they have to ask the rules they are not allowed to play. As Marc Segar wrote (1997),

> When people break these unwritten rules, sometimes they get away with it, but usually they who break informal rules are made to suffer informal punishments. These punishments may include being laughed at, being treated as a less important person or being isolated.

> The most difficult thing about being autistic (or having Asperger syndrome) is that so many people expect you to know

these rules and live by them, as they do, even though no-one has told you what these rules are. There is no doubt that this is extremely unfair, but unfortunately most people don't see it that way as they don't understand your problem.

I will always remember one afternoon in the locker room during the sixth form. Some foolery changed imperceptibly into a game of tag. Our well rehearsed sophistication melted away and we became children again. The game ended as suddenly as it began. But while the others rearranged their features and recovered their composure I burst out in all innocence, 'What shall we play next!'

The looks I got! Those eyes still speak to me with sneering contempt. 'Play! We do not play! That was an accident. Do not mention it again. We are 16 years old and Masters of the Universe. WE DO NOT PLAY!'

How many times do young people with autism feel all the pain and confusion at moments like that without the benefit of understanding why?

Changes to themselves

It is bad enough that the world is changing. But, while you may rant against your friends for their betrayal in growing up and growing away from you, you can always turn your back on the world and concentrate on your own interests. Until, that is, you start to change.

One young man told me that sex was too complicated and too messy so he had decided to shut it out of his mind. That was at 12. At 14 he discovered that his body would not let him. Then he decided that he had enough pubic hair but it would not stop growing. It is not just the physical changes. My son does not like the strange new thoughts he is having, like what will life hold for him after I die?

Around this time teenagers with Asperger syndrome become acutely aware of peer group pressure and the need to conform and belong to the social group. But just when their desire for socialisation is at its height their peer group is absorbed by their own insecurity and at their most unsympathetic. Everyone else wants to belong as well and the safest bet is to have nothing to do with the nerds and geeks and social misfits. Indeed, based on the old premise of 'tuppence ha'penny looking down on tuppence' the socially inadequate are likely to seek out the child with autism and torment them to bolster their own self-esteem.

Adults change

Children with autism often prefer the company of adults. They are safer than the peer group, more secure in themselves, predictable and set in their ways. But even they seem affected by adolescence.

It may be hard to imagine, but some of the most rebellious teenagers with autism are those who have the strongest desire to please. They become frustrated because they cannot make sense of our expectations of them.

We expect them to grow up and act their age and they do try. They observe their peers. They learn what teenagers do. Then they do it! Unfortunately they have not learned the discretion and self-preservation that the ordinary teenager brings to their acts of rebellion. Knowing how far you can go; pushing so far and no further are skills our children lack. What we get instead is full scale revolution.

People with autism spend a good deal of their lives being made painfully aware of their shortcomings. At 14 my son is sick to the back teeth with lectures and criticisms. And I am as guilty as anybody.

After one particular incident where I got it spectacularly wrong he said to me, 'You messed up big time there, Dad...'

'Yes,' I said, 'and so did you.'

'But I am autistic. What's your excuse?' came the reply.

CHAPTER 10

Adult Life

Once you are over the initial reaction to diagnosis, whether you were devastated or relieved, most parents want to know what the future holds. This is also important for administrators who often have little idea about the scale of services and provision that people with autism might require in the course of their lifetime.

Now it may seem foolish to attempt to describe the possible outcomes for a disorder that is so wide ranging and variable in its effects. But some things can be said with reasonable confidence.

Autism is for life

Autism is a lifelong condition. Like the high-wire artiste the person with autism may, with practise, get very good at performing their balancing act and perform with such consummate ease that a stranger would be hard pressed to detect anything special in what they do. But, again like the high-wire artiste, the person with autism knows they are one step from disaster. Even if they fall less frequently as they get older and wiser, it is still a long way down when they do fall. We also have to remember that it is a long way to climb back up again. And not all people with autism make it back to the top. Even the most able person who perfects the art of imitating so called 'normal behaviour' can break under the strain. Mental breakdown, depression, suicide are the sometimes tragic consequences of our failure to make life easier for them.

Some may be less willing to risk all in exchange for acceptance. So they may present as less well adapted to society while being more at ease with themselves. But, whichever path they happen to be on at the time, all people with autism will require some form of support throughout their lives.

Liane Holliday Willey (1999) has vividly described how, although her symptoms are now quite mild, she is literally 'pretending to be normal' and sometimes feels as though she is on the brink of a precipice waiting to plunge into the abyss below. Her support is provided by her husband and children. Others may find their social impairment precludes such a solution and will need access to self-help groups, therapists, sheltered employment and group living arrangements.

For many adults with autism their main support is provided by their parents. It should not have to be. If they cannot be helped into independent life styles while we parents are still alive and able to support the transition how do social services expect them to cope with independence if it is thrust upon them after we are dead?

Another issue arises when a young person with autism attains majority. If they need help managing their affairs parents are the most obvious choice. But even though we often continue to take responsibility we have no legal rights regarding our adult offspring. If we want to make financial provision for them how are we to prevent the unscrupulous from exploiting their social naiveté in order to cheat them? What happens if we dispute a decision of the adult social services division concerning our child's future? How can we make a will and be confident that our child's inheritance will be managed in his best interests? These are questions that go beyond my level of knowledge and expertise. They affect a much wider layer of adults with disabilities than just those on the autistic spectrum. They are matters of immediate concern to many parents and will not go away.

Adult life promises to be the most interesting stage yet in our journey with Matthew. We are not too sure what to expect but one or two signs are emerging.

Matthew is growing up fit and healthy. He is unlikely to smoke or become a regular drinker. His obsession with health has some benefits. He likes to work out and will probably live for a very long time. Some people with autism do have a range of co-morbid disorders. But in general people with autism are no more or less likely to suffer from life threatening illnesses than anyone else.

Sometimes obsessive behaviour or irrational dietary habits make self-management of diseases like epilepsy or diabetes problematic and there are risks of self-harm associated with the tendency to greater depression among people with autism. Apart from that the probability is that the adult with autism will outlive their caregivers and most of their peer group as well.

So any adult services that are put in place need long-term planning and adult services do need to be put in place. As I mentioned earlier, parents should not be expected to assume the burden of adult care. And the more independence the adult with autism can achieve the easier the transition that will have to be made after the parents have died.

Avoiding unfortunate situations

'On Monday December 13, 1999 ABC News 20/20 aired a segment that focused on an autistic man's false confession to bank robbery charges.' (Debbaudt 1999)

This section takes its name from Dennis Debbaudt's web site. Dennis, a private investigator with an autistic teenager, has written books about the risk of unfortunate outcomes for people with autism in their dealings with the police and lectured to law enforcement agencies across the USA. When I wrote to him about an individual with autism who had been imprisoned by a judge who seemed to have no understanding of autism he replied that these cases were increasing. His mail box used to get one a month. Now he gets one a week.

People with autism do get into trouble with the police. But it is often the case that their social naiveté leads to misunderstandings and mistakes. It is almost axiomatic that a person with autism is honest and law abiding, sometimes to a fault. So they are sometimes rather blunt in their dealings with authority figures. If a blustering nincompoop of a traffic cop pulls up a man with high functioning autism for some trivial violation he may not appreciate being told in no uncertain terms what that person thinks of his mental capacities, especially if it is true!

The case that Dennis refers to is more serious. People with autism are used to being told they are wrong. They are brought up to trust authority figures and accept their version of events. They spend a lot of time working out what people expect of them and doing their best to comply. If such a person is mistakenly suspected and arrested they may either confess to please their interrogators or react so violently to the injustice of it all that they finish up facing even more serious charges.

The answer, as always, is to increase autism awareness within the community and I thoroughly recommend Dennis's web site to anyone with concerns in this area.

Investing in autism

Another sign from Matthew which I find confirmed by my correspondence with adults with autism is that greater maturity enhances self-control and awareness of his strengths and limitations. This should not be taken to mean that autism is a problem that children grow out of, thus negating the need for services. Adults who are ignored by the system or denied support can become victims of drug and alcohol abuse, and leave a trail of broken relationships, sometimes with offspring for others to care for. They often cannot keep a job and may descend into homelessness and welfare dependency.

Once they understand their problem and come to terms with living in a world that is both confusing and unsympathetic many become advocates for the autistic community. They become writers, consultants, teachers. One example is Andrew Walker, recently profiled in the Guardian (Jan 4 2000). Five years ago, undiagnosed, he was alienated from his family, divorced, suicidal. Now 40, he is in a stable relationship, studying for a PhD in autism and determined to 'make things better for the next generation'.

The point is that investment in people with Asperger syndrome pays dividends. By and large they want to be useful, they want to belong. They are conscientious employees. They are law abiding citizens. They can often achieve independent, productive life styles. It is when support is lacking or withdrawn that they become casualties, unemployable, dependent on the state.

The third thing that I have noticed is how diverse the personalities of adults with autism are. Abrasive, apologetic, sympathetic to others, self-centred, shy, confident. Just like the rest of us, with strengths and weaknesses. Each personality emerges unique, often after immense struggles. And, when you read the life stories, there is often very little clue in a person's childhood about the way they will turn out.

One young woman with autism described two children, identical in every respect. They have the same problems. They inhabit the same environment. But they react in different ways and their conditions are interpreted differently. One is labelled autistic, the other is gifted but odd. In other words, there is no point in trying to pick the winners or match services to projected outcomes. The only way to pick a winner is to back them all.

CHAPTER II

Myths and Insights

The popular image of autism is slowly being corrected as more accurate pieces appear in the mainstream media. But a number of myths persist. Like all myths they have their basis in fact and extracting this kernel of truth can help to dispose of the myths and deepen our understanding.

I cannot tell a lie

People with autism can be honest to a fault. Everyone has stood in line at the supermarket and squirmed with embarrassment when their toddler cries out, 'Why is that lady so fat?' Other parents in the line smile and nod to each other in that knowing 'been there; done that' manner. The fat lady turns rounds and melts before the innocent gaze of your child. You exchange some inane pleasantries and the matter ends without incident.

But, while this may be acceptable and even endearing in a typical two year old, imagine the same scenario with a six foot tall, teenage son in the starring role! It is tempting to regard this as the downside of the higher moral purpose with which people with autism are imbued. One of Matthew's assessments even states that children with Asperger syndrome 'always tell the truth, regardless of the consequences or other people's feelings'. The reality is somewhat more complex.

There is rule bound honesty. I will always remember standing on the bottom step of the school bus clutching my penny bus fare and crying with anguish because the conductor had not collected my fare, instead of heading across the road to the sweet shop like my friends. I can claim no higher moral purpose. I was given the penny to pay my bus fare. I had to do it. But once inside the school I found some model soldiers so attractive that I just had to have them and so I took them home with me. Fear and embarrassment prevented me from confessing when the loss was investigated the next day. But I knew I had broken a rule and so great was my shame that if the teacher had asked me directly, 'Did you take the soldiers?' I would have blurted out the truth.

Social naiveté can also be mistaken for honesty. The child tells the truth because they don't know any better. They have no reason to lie. Good manners, the feelings of others, imagining the possible consequences for themselves — if these considerations are not available to them they will blurt out the truth. Matthew tries to compliment me on my cooking. He will say something like, 'This dinner is nice, for a change' and wonder why I am not pleased.

But if it suits their purpose they are just as capable of deception as the rest of us. It is just that in their innocence they see the need for deception less often.

Recently Matthew decided to stop taking his medication. He did not tell us. In fact he actively deceived us, not very well as it turns out. We detected his deception after a week and he confessed immediately. This reinforces the point that lying is a difficult but not impossible skill for people with autism to acquire.

His reasons for doing so and deceiving us reminded me of the tunnel/bridge dilemma discussed in the next chapter. Matthew knew that he had problems. He knew that the medication helped him to handle those problems, just as the bridge offered a route around his traumatic tantrum behaviour. But at what cost? Was he missing the point here? Did the tablets deal with the symptoms while failing to address the cause? Did they ease the pain but also cost him 'the pleasure, joy, warmth of heart and relief' that came after the pain? Were they taking away a part of himself, his identity? He had to find out. And so he lied because it was important to him to discover a more important truth.

People with autism are self-absorbed

A problem reported time and again by parents struggling to get a diagnosis is the comment from professionals that, 'He is not autistic. He is too interested in other people'.

People with autism can be very interested in other people. It is just that they have great difficulty in working out what makes us tick and relating to us on our terms. In my experience of children with autism from across the spectrum they are often very sensitive to the intensity of the emotional atmosphere around them even if they are not so good at reading those emotions and responding appropriately.

Thus, when Katie's hamster died she was very upset. Matthew understood this much. His sister was sad and that made him feel uncomfortable. When he was sad he liked to cheer himself up with jokes so he started to clown around in order to cheer her up. Of course, she was not impressed and turned on him for being insensitive to her grief. So he got upset at her ingratitude because he was only trying to help.

This sort of gaffe often leads people to believe that people with autism are selfish. And they are in the limited sense that they judge situations according to the impact on themselves. This is partly because they do have difficulty imagining what other people are thinking or feeling. But partly it is based on the very real observation that in many situations people share the same emotions. So if you are feeling frightened, happy, embarrassed etc. the chances are that those around you are feeling the same emotions. So they respond to what the evidence suggests others must be feeling. The social instinct is there. The drive to empathy is there. It is just damaged or impaired and gives the person misleading data.

It is sometimes very hard to remember this when you are being driven to distraction by the apparent insensitivity and selfishness of the person with autism. But if you can distance yourself just try and remember that your behaviour is probably just as incomprehensible and frustrating to them.

Bursting the autistic bubble

The bubble refers to another myth about autism; namely that there is a 'normal' person inside whose attempts to relate to the world are distorted by their autistic shell. According to this myth there are autistic behaviours like rocking and flapping and all the other stereotypes and other, more recognizable behaviours that are miraculously free of all autistic connotations. These are supposed to represent the 'real' person inside and sometimes this 'real' person is supposed to shine through.

This sort of myth is no help at all. Any evidence of autism is seen as a problem to be eliminated. Even people with high functioning autism rely on a lot of so called stereotypical behaviour such as hand flapping, spinning and rocking to help them concentrate, for emotional release and to cope with stressful situations. It serves no purpose to suppress these behaviours. All that happens is that you increase the pressure and the levels of stress. On the other hand all evidence of 'normal' functioning is taken as evidence that the 'treatment' is working. We are 'breaking through' the shell; 'rescuing' the child within. This model is quite pernicious. The person with autism is seen as a helpless victim who has to be saved. Every 'success' is down to the dedication of the therapist. The victim is given no credit at all and is even supposed to be grateful for his or her 'cure'.

Thankfully this point of view is largely discredited among therapists but tends to linger in the popular consciousness. This is a source of much frustration and anger to parents who try and explain their child's syndrome to uncomprehending friends and relatives only to be told:

'You cannot let him win all the time.'

'He is dominating your life.'

'He just needs a firm hand.'

'If I had him for a fortnight, I would soon sort him out.'

'He just needs to know who's the boss.'

'He cannot hide behind his autism all his life.'

'There is no excuse for that sort of behaviour.'

It is in fact impossible to separate the 'normal' from the 'autistic' behaviours in this way. The person with autism has a fundamental impairment of social cognition that recent studies suggest is linked to atypical patterns of brain behaviour and structure (Abell *et al.* 1999). So called 'normal' behaviours often represent real achievements by people with high functioning autism. There are things they are good at. But their autism contributes to every aspect of their personality, good, bad and neutral.

So the idea that autism is a handicapping condition that operates at the interface between the affected individual and the world is misleading. To use a computer analogy, it is not the input/output bus that is at fault. The central processing unit is differently wired. One person with autism argued that they were an Apple Mac trying to emulate a Windows PC and not just a faulty Windows machine screwing up in a PC world.

'That's not autism. All kids do that'

Remarks like this may be meant to reassure but the message can be hurtful. It means that others do not take your problems seriously. They seem to be saying there is nothing wrong with your child so whatever the problem is it must be your fault.

Aunt and uncle may dismiss your worries about late talking. After six months of therapy and a lot of hard work by you and your child they come for another visit and take all the credit when he greets them. 'See, I told you he would speak given time.'

What people forget is that in young children it is hard to distinguish between evidence of autism and typical toddler behaviour. That is why we use specialist diagnostic tools finely tuned for the task. I have a poor ear for music so it is no use my telling Katie that 'it sounds all right to me' when she is practising to get a piano piece just right. If only Joe Public would develop an ear for autism before regaling us with opinions and advice.

As your child gets older it gets harder. You have to be very careful how you tell a person with autism when they are wrong. Low self-esteem is a common problem among people with high functioning autism. Constructive criticism is a difficult concept to grasp. Even the most well intentioned advice can be interpreted as a put down. Sometimes, when I attempt to correct Matthew, he reacts as if I were condemning the whole core of his being. But people still delight in telling me that all teenagers are difficult. I know that. I also know that there is a qualitative difference between Matthew's problems and those of his NT peers. Katie suffers from teenage angst and I offer support and understanding. Matthew suffers from teenage angst and I suffer with him.

Aint misbehavin'

The young person with autism is quite capable of misbehaving or breaking the social rules as well as simply failing to understand them. I have already shown how it is meaningless to attempt to ascribe actions to the normal or autistic parts of their personality. Playing loud music late at night; refusing to tidy your room; slobbing out all day on the sofa with your games console and then finding a hundred things to do just before bedtime: the young person with autism indulges in all of these but adds a specific autistic slant. Often a typical teenager acts without thinking and is willing to stand corrected when you point out the impact of their behaviour on others. People with autism rarely act without thinking and will resist all attempts to change their behaviour by appeals to reason with clear cut arguments to demonstrate the correctness of their position.

'I am only playing my stereo so loud because the music helps me to calm down.' 'If you don't want me to calm down that is fine. I will come downstairs and have a real tantrum. Is that what you want?'

Often they are not misbehaving. It is just that a teenager's capacity to annoy expands to match our middle aged propensity to be annoyed. I have observed this phenomenon in myself now that I have an NT teenage daughter and a son with high functioning autism. Say we are planning to go somewhere. Katie spends days making lists – what to wear, what to take etc. and generally exhausts my patience by going on and on about it. Matthew, on the other hand, needs to know precisely what our plans are but does nothing to contribute until five minutes before we are due to leave when he delivers his agenda – he needs a clean shirt, a shower, he has not packed his bag yet. I have not seen it written in any diagnostic criteria but it seems to me that there is a direct link between a person with high functioning autism's need for structure and organization and their own total lack of organisational skills.

Beam me up, Scottie!

Many people with autism are Star Trek enthusiasts and often their favourite character is Data, the android who struggles to work out what it is to be human or Spock, the Vulcan whose ancestors chose logic over emotion as the guiding force for their planet, unlike us sentimental, emotionally unstable humans.

There is a myth, often encouraged by some people with autism, that they are alien or android-like figures struggling to comprehend us lesser mortals. It is true that the person with autism can sometimes feel like an 'Anthropologist on Mars,' to quote the title employed by Oliver Sacks in his essay on Temple Grandin. But they are most definitely part of the human race whether they like it or not. Autism is a disability which makes extra demands on those who have it. They may find strength in adversity. But the adversity that comes with being autistic is a very real test of that strength. Autism is a disabling condition and not the next step in human evolution.

Thinking like a human

Matthew sometimes pretends to be normal. He acts as he thinks we expect him to act, even when he finds it uncomfortable and unnatural. It is rather like trying to have a conversation in French while thinking in English and simultaneously translating your thoughts into French at the same time as you translate what you hear into English.

It would be a lot easier if you could think and speak in French at the same time. Matthew has been trying a similar trick with neuro-typical behaviour; *being normal* instead of *pretending to be normal*. **Pretending** involves working out our expectations of him and trying to act accordingly. **Being** is a higher risk activity in which he imagines what we would do in that situation and tries to act like us.

Recently on holiday we went to see a fireworks display. Matthew arranged a time and a place to meet us 'in case I lose you' and promptly disappeared. At 10.30pm we turned up at the appointed place – no Matthew. 11.00 – still no Matthew. 11.15 and we are getting worried. If Matthew says something he does it. He is usually very rule bound. We inform the police and Dee takes Katie back to the youth hostel while I wait with growing anxiety.

Meanwhile a large outdoor screen is showing a movie. Just after midnight the movie ends and Matthew comes back to the rendezvous totally unconcerned. His explanation was that we had commented earlier on what a good film it was so when he arrived at the rendezvous at exactly 10.30 and we were not there he assumed we had gone to see the film, went in search of us and promptly lost himself in the crowd. So he watched the film, confident that we were doing the same and would meet as arranged, albeit two hours late.

Mild autism?

Asperger syndrome is sometimes referred to by the popular media as a mild form of autism. What they mean is that the person with Asperger syndrome does not have the additional impairments of a person with autism and associated learning disabilities. On the surface they may appear to be mildly affected by their autism. But who can tell what turmoil threatens below the surface?

A person with autism and an IQ in the Mensa range is just as liable to tantrum behaviour or panic attacks as any other person with autism. The fact that they often give vent to graphic verbal descriptions of their fears, frustrations and hates at these times can make such events even more distressing for those in the firing line than the kicking and biting versions of their less able autistic cousins on the spectrum. I have experienced both and would rather be bitten than subject to violent verbal abuse.

Matthew once told me that he wished he had been 'properly' autistic like a boy he had met during an activity week with Riding for the Disabled. This lad more closely matched the criteria for classical autism of the Kanner type. Matthew is in his own way equally autistic but envied him because the other boy was blissfully unaware of his condition and not prey to the same doubts and fears that beset people with Asperger syndrome. They are often acutely aware of their shortcomings and difficulties and rail against the unfairness of it all. They struggle to understand our world but receive scant sympathy and understanding in return. Many acquire additional conditions such as depression because of the constant worry and pressure they are exposed to. Threats of suicide are not uncommon and, sadly, in some cases they are acted upon. Mild autism? I don't think so.

CHAPTER 12

Challenging Behaviour

Challenging behaviour can take many forms. The person may be violent, destructive, self-injurious. They may have really annoying or antisocial habits which no amount of threats or cajolery can dent. Tantrums, manic highs and dark depressions all combine to form a roller coaster ride in which others are dragged along in the wake of the person with autism. This behaviour can seem deliberate and manipulative or malicious in intent. But this is no more so than is the case with a drowning man whose flailing arms threaten the lives of his would be rescuers. In moments of panic when they have temporarily lost the battle for stability in their lives they are indeed 'drowning not waving', and need our help and not our admonitions.

Asperger syndrome, temper tantrums and panic attacks – what it is like

Carry it on, lapping it up. I didn't want it to end. It's like when you're eating a sweet. When it's there I enjoy it and make it last as long as possible when it's there. But you act and try to be normal and you don't notice the sweet's not there. And when Dad says, 'Sorry,' I say, 'I'll think about it,' and at last I got Dad under my power so to speak.

There's a tunnel and a bridge. The tunnel leads through a temper tantrum or a panic attack to where there's immense pleasure and warmth in the heart and relief. 'The bridge leads away from that but still giving pleasure and relief?' After going through, the pleasure and relief and warmth in the heart seem greater because of the wider gap between struggle to get through the tunnel and to get the pleasure and relief and feeling warmth in the heart.

Once I'm a metre (so to speak) in the tunnel I want to carry on. It's like a massage but the other way round. In a massage you're working. By massaging you get pleasure immediately. But when you're in the tunnel you have to work first, then the pleasure, joy, warmth of heart and relief.

To get to the end of the tunnel, where there's pleasure, joy, relief and warmth in my heart and anyone trying to stop me will be like a challenge trying to stop me getting to those pleasures at the end of the tunnel. And if they do succeed in stopping me then I just return to the agitated state I was before I entered the tunnel. Unless you stop me in time, before it is too late, and direct me to the bridge.

Also by taking away completely the temper tantrums and the panic attacks completely, it will be like banning football completely from a football fanatic or, putting it better, it will be like taking away someone's heart.

Matthew wrote this account when he was 12. I find it instructive because it suggests that even the most negative behaviours can have a positive role. It is obvious from what he writes that the autistic tantrum for Matthew has never been an indulgence. It is a serious business that takes its toll on him as well as us. But on balance its benefits in terms of restoring mental peace make it worth the pain and suffering, 'the work' as he describes it.

This was written at a particularly bad time in Matthew's life. Secondary school transfer had been a disaster and he felt his life was falling apart. Tantrum behaviour, while not exactly putting him in control, did mean that the world had to deal with him on his terms and could not ignore him. I had to say 'sorry' for example in an attempt to defuse the situation. He knew that there were alternatives to the tantrum tunnel like the bridge –

looking for alternative solutions. But would they have the same cathartic effect?

I had originally suggested the bridge to Matthew as an analogy for looking for ways round his problems instead of going through them in the tunnel. He has since told me that the problem with the bridge was that it was *my* bridge. It was *my* solution to *his* problems. He did not trust it. He thought it meant ignoring his problems. The tantrum tunnel was hard and dangerous but at least it met his problems head on. He now talks of building his own bridge, finding his own ways to cope with his problems and not just being expected to take everything I say on trust. As Matthew says now

> *You always want to solve my problems and I think that is it.*
> *Problems over. That is what school tried to do. But the problems*
> *are there forever, continuously. I have to learn to cope with them.*
> *You cannot take them away from me. Even though I do not want*
> *your solutions I still need your help to find ways to cope and help*
> *me through. And hopefully it becomes automatic, a part of me and*
> *I can cope without thinking about it.*

This helps to explain the apparently irrational adherence to maladaptive patterns of behaviour by high functioning individuals with autism who 'ought' to know better. We have no problems accepting the punishing schedules that athletes impose upon themselves. 'No Pain, No Gain' has even entered the language to justify such behaviour. Might not a person with autism take a similar view of their own punishing regimes? Once established, patterns of behaviour can be very hard to unlearn, especially if they are associated with eventual positive effects, the 'pleasures at the end of the tunnel'.

Parents, teachers and therapists may tout alternatives with the promise of more gain for less pain. But the old cliché, 'better the devil you know...' holds immense power over people with autism for whom knowledge is a hard won and precious commodity. They can be rather like the man clinging to the wreckage who refuses all attempts to entice him into the life-raft, saying, 'You won't catch me in a boat again. I don't trust them. The last one I went in sank.'

Meltdown

Every person with autism knows what it is like when accumulated stresses of the day become too much to bear. Then the slightest provocation takes you over your critical mass. Parents know it as well. Often we are the ones who inadvertently provide the chance remark at the end of a hard day at school that provokes meltdown as our offspring go ballistic.

Schools often do not understand the psychological strain of holding yourself in readiness for the hidden blow. And if that blow never comes your anxiety increases. Until you get home and explode. Then school responds with, 'Well he copes well enough in class.' One Educational Psychologist thought it was a cause for satisfaction that Matthew's behaviour was contained at school. He did not understand that school was not coping with Matthew. Matthew was in fact under immense strain coping with school.

Many parents would agree with Tony Attwood's description of the high school/secondary school as a mine field in a jungle populated by predators (Attwood 1999). The pupil with autism not only worries about their own behaviour, making a mistake that will start an explosion. They are also likely to be ambushed by bullies when they least expect it. So they come home and vent on us.

> *Even with it written out in a report the school does not really get it that my son, yes, has problems, but the way he was treated really hurt him emotionally and permanently. I also was told for years, 'be glad he can feel safe enough to express himself to you'. Well, yes, I'm glad he knows I love him and try so darn hard to help in his life, school, etc. But it really gets depressing sometimes to be lashed out at and hear a lot of really angry rants from a ten year old.*

I cannot claim to be any kind of expert, but my experience with schools in the UK might help. We had terrible trouble with our eight year old son – extreme anger and rage, self-harm, depression, suicide threats etc. before diagnosis with AS in January this year, so we changed schools. It made all the difference to have a proper diagnosis and a new start in school which came at the same time of crisis. The bad experiences kind of built up from day to day at his old school. The effect was accumulative and irreversible. There came a time where his negative feelings about the school escalated so badly, over Xmas last year, that we simply quit the school, with no new school to go to. We were lucky to find any new state school to take him. My experience is that my son had very bad feelings and anger directed against particular teachers and individuals which would not change; this got worse from day to day.

This whole rage thing is fascinating and so vital to us. The comment about needing a classroom where they are accepted is right on the mark for us. Last year he had a teacher who, I'm sure, had a good heart, but was very regimented and controlled in her thinking. Her way or no way. He was a wreck and so were we by the end of the year. This year he has the most wonderful teacher who sees where he is coming from and draws the good out of him. To say it's like night and day would be an understatement.

Responding to challenging behaviour

When dealing with challenging behaviour the hardest thing to do is not to be challenged by it. As a parent I find it more difficult to ignore the gauntlet when it is thrown down my son than I do as a teacher when dealing with the confrontational behaviour of a pupil. But I know that I ought to ignore it. To follow Matthew's analogy with the tunnel, I may tell myself that I am just going in a little way to bring him out and show him the bridge. But it does not always work out that way. I have followed him all the way in and come out the other side. Unfortunately for me I did not get 'the pleasure and relief and feeling of warmth in the heart' that Matthew experiences. Instead I felt guilty, ashamed and exhausted.

If it is too late to bring the youngster out of the tunnel how do we intervene without making a bad situation worse? Often we cannot. Providing they are not endangering themselves or those around them, letting it take its course is often a good idea. This sort of behaviour can be quite scary for them and it helps to have a calm and confident, non-confrontational presence nearby.

Sometimes we can intervene successfully. Some people find a really tight hug or an all enveloping squeeze can help to calm them in moments of extreme panic. This is not the same as the 'holding therapy' that aroused controversy a few years ago when you were supposed to hold your child against his will in order to break through the autism to the child inside. The comfort some people gain from physical pressure has more in common with the brushing and joint compression that occupational therapists use with subjects who have an excessive degree of tactile defensiveness.

Before you dive in with the hugs, a word of caution. If the person is feeling angry with you or identifies you with their distress they are not going to appreciate your intervention! I was the nearest when one young lad fell and cracked his head. So I was to blame and got a right clawing when I rushed to pick him up. The second person on the scene got all the love and cuddles while he forgot his hurt and complained about 'bad Stanton'.

I am getting better at divining when Matthew wants comfort and when he wants to be left alone. Just remember there is nothing worse than someone trying to cheer you up when you are 'enjoying' a good sulk. Make sure your interventions are welcome and withdraw if they are not.

If you are a professional make sure that guidelines for all physical interventions are clearly described in the relevant policy documents for your institution and that you are certified to use them with clients. Parents are particularly concerned about the confusion over whether restraints are used out of a duty of care or in order to gain compliance and that duly authorized personnel have received adequate training to handle their children safely when necessary.

It is up to us to identify those situations that provoke challenging behaviour and minimize their occurrence. It is also as well to remember that the person with autism may feel that they are merely responding to our challenging behaviour. You cannot be simultaneously part of the solution and part of the problem – not in their scheme of things, anyway. In those situations it is better to hand over to someone else and ignore our personal need to prove that it was not our fault, that it was just a misunderstanding etc.

We are used to the idea that someone can be struck dumb with amazement or speechless with rage. The person with autism experiences a more fundamental impairment. Even the most able person loses access to communication skills during periods of stress or anxiety. The person with autism may 'forget' that other people are not mind readers, an illusion we un-wittingly foster by our ability to read a situation and imagine what someone else might be thinking. So not only are they in extreme distress; they may also become very angry with us for not intuiting why and then failing to respond appropriately to the need that they believe their behaviour was communicating.

Of course, sometimes the person with autism is plain wrong and needs to be helped or corrected whether they like it or not. Violence associated with tantrum behaviour cannot be tolerated. Nor can self-injurious behaviour. But we have to use a tool like behaviour modification with care. It can be very powerful. We should never use it to get the person to tolerate the intolerable and habituate them to distress so that they no longer react.

I remember a lecture many years ago when behaviour modifi-cation was the 'latest thing' in special education and there were check lists and programmes for everything. My faith in the technique was tempered by a tale from our lecturer, John

Mortlock. He warned us always to look for and eliminate external causes of behaviour before using psychological methods such as behaviour modification. He quoted two examples of violent rages and head banging that failed to respond to a behavioural programme. The first turned out to be caused by impacted wisdom teeth. The second had an untreated abscess in his ear! Always eliminate the obvious.

One of the most effective ways to eliminate challenging behaviour is not to intervene head on to extinguish it but to redirect by teaching the person more socially acceptable methods of modifying our behaviour or their environment to remove the source of panic or anger.

Communication breakdown is far and away the most likely cause for many outbursts. Whatever the system – words or signs or a symbol system – the youngster needs to learn how to use it effectively to send as well as receive messages. 'Stop now.' 'No more talking.' 'I need a hug now.' 'Time out.' How many times could the effective receipt of such messages by us forestall tantrums, meltdown and extreme distress in the person with autism? So one of the most effective means of dealing with challenging behaviour is to teach appropriate communication skills to the person with autism and to teach carers, teachers and others to understand their communication system and respond appropriately.

CHAPTER 13

Mind Your Language

Story tellers from the ancient oral traditions used repetition in their epic tales to keep the attention of a large and sometimes less than ruly audience and ensure that everyone got the point. It reminds me of the advice I was given by a seasoned campaigner on the art of public speaking. 'For the introduction: tell them what you are going to say. Then say it. In conclusion: remind them what you've said.'

In principle this is a good method to adopt with people with autism, many of whom are better at processing visual than auditory information. Speech is a transitory medium and meaning is easily missed or confused. So repetition seems to be in order. But the person with autism may have a different perspective. There are many ways that verbal communication can go wrong.

They may not realize you are talking to them

If I say to my class, 'Everybody sit down please', and the child with autism ignores me, the rest of the class notice that John is acting weird again. I say, 'John, did you hear me.' 'Yes,' he replies and carries on with his activity. Some of the class are sniggering now. 'John!' I raise my voice. He looks surprised. 'Sit down now, please!' John sits down with an expression that suggests, 'No need to shout. Why didn't you say so in the first place?'

This is not deliberate insubordination. John does not know he is being addressed unless he hears his name. So he does not respond to 'Everybody' but he will respond if I attract his attention first by saying, 'John, sit down, please. Everybody, sit down like John, please.'

They may miss out on non verbal clues to meaning

Attention on its own does not guarantee understanding. The person with autism often has to consciously think about body language, facial expressions, intonation and all the other non verbal elements of communication while trying to decipher the meaning of your words. This is less of a problem in a classroom where the teacher is lecturing the class. Communication is largely one way. The teacher imparts information. But many sessions are far more dynamic than that. There is give and take, turn taking, subtle alteration of tone or content to take account of the listener's response. This is when the person with autism is liable to lose the thread and become stressed.

Too much stress can overload the system

At a TEACCH seminar I attended in 1996, Gary Mesibov described how Donna Williams refers to 'untouchable sound' when stress causes speech to degenerate into a meaningless noise. This escalates into sensory overload as other senses are affected. 'Meaning drops out of what I am seeing. I become meaning blind and meaning deaf.' Note that meaning is lost but she is still aware of the sensory inputs bombarding her, until 'sensory shutdown' which she describes as being like dying as all sensory inputs are blocked out.

Temple Grandin describes similar problems with communication. She starts to get confused or upset. People offer words of help which only make matters worse by adding to the sensory over-stimulation.

It is important to remember that once this stage has been reached even the most supportive words, given with the best of intentions, only add to the babble and can make matters worse.

Hearing is not always reliable

In the animation 'A is for Autism', first shown on TV and now available on video (Channel 4 1992), young people talk about how their hearing sometimes plays tricks on them. Like a badly tuned radio, the volume comes in and out of its own volition, the signal fades or starts to break up, the sound balance is distorted so that a ticking clock becomes excruciatingly loud while the person across the table is mouthing away but no sound can be heard. Voices rise and merge into a cacophony of sound or become barely audible whispers. Crunching leaves hurt the ears.

If the child is afraid of dogs the distant sound of a dog barking may overwhelm their attention so that while tuned in to this potentially important information (Is the dog getting closer?) they tune out all other distractions, including the voice of the teacher, or the sound of the car bearing down on them as they are crossing the road.

Some people report problems with the barely imperceptible hum of fluorescent lighting so common in institutional settings such as schools and offices. One child even complained of the noise of the butterfly wings in his garden! On the other hand sounds they enjoy can be equally disconcerting for the rest of us. At one meeting I heard the story of a young man who liked the sound of squealing brakes so much that he took to leaping out in front of moving cars!

Problems with meaning

Old map makers filled in the gaps in their knowledge of the world with 'Terra Incognita' or 'Here be Dragons and Monsters' etc. People with autism often carry similar cognitive maps in their heads. What they do know is entered on the map with painstaking accuracy. But the areas of ignorance can be filled with terrors for them. Here indeed be dragons and monsters.

Most of us are probably unaware of our cognitive maps. We navigate through life 'on the fly' subconsciously redrawing our maps and reforming our cognitive schemata. There will be times when we consciously grapple with new concepts and are able to transform existing cognitive structures in the light of fresh learning and experience. These will be memorable experiences for us. We may refer to being on a learning curve at such times. Imagine, if you will, such intensive and conscious learning activity as an everyday experience and you are half way to understanding the pressures on a person with autism.

Our handiest tool of thought is language. It is the intellectual equivalent of the lever or the wheel. For the person with autism it is a different story. Language is a rule not a tool.

'In the beginning was the word and the word was made flesh' has literal meaning. Language defines and limits reality rather than emerging from and expressing aspects of reality. Vygotsky, in his seminal work, *Thought and Language* (1962) recounts the tale of two Russian peasants marvelling at the night sky. One is full of praise for modern science and the ability of Soviet astronomers to measure the distances to the stars. His comrade thinks a while and then pronounces, 'Yes, that is all very well, but what I don't understand is how they discovered the stars' names.'

Vygotsky also recalls a tale by Dostoyevsky in which the hero follows a group of workmen down the street. Their entire conversation consists of swear words. Yet they are used with such variation of tone that within their shared context the workmen were able to conduct an entire conversation with perfect understanding. I do not know how it would translate into English but I do remember that on my first day as a dockside labourer, after a day of curses and hard labour an old docker came up to me and with great tenderness told me to 'Fuck off now, son.'

These twin attributes of language – extracting meaning from experience and our ability to alter meaning to fit the context so that 'Fuck off' becomes a term of endearment – often seem to be reversed in people with autism. Language imposes meaning rather than being a tool to extract meaning from the situation.

Taking things literally

Excessive literality can have devastating consequences. At a very basic level, when you tell a youngster to sit down, are they ever going to be allowed to stand up again? When you say, 'Don't eat the last chocolate biscuit!' what are you do to when they turn round and say, 'Right! I will never eat again!' Not with sarcasm or irony, mind you, but with extreme literality, because you said, 'Don't eat...' and that is when they stopped listening, or, to be more accurate, stopped decoding your words. At a more advanced level the subtle consequences of the over literal approach to language can also have far reaching consequences.

When Matthew was seven he was asked by a speech therapist, 'What is your favourite story?' He replied, 'I do not know because there are hundreds and hundreds of stories in the library and Daddy has not read them all to me yet.' Six years later he came home from school and asked me, 'What are all the laws?' It turned out that he had a homework assignment to write about the three laws he would change if he had the power. Matthew took this very seriously indeed. In order to choose the right laws to change he would need to know about all of them.

Taking things literally is a common feature of autism. It can serve as a reminder to us to mind our language. I remember a tale of a girl on her first day at school. She arrived and was told 'to wait here for the present.' She went home in tears because she *had* waited but nobody had given her a present (Donaldson 1978).

With Matthew, anxiety about exams has always been a problem. His teachers have been made aware of this and we have all tried to reassure him in the past with expressions like, 'Just do your best.' We actually meant to communicate, 'Do your worst. We know you are worried, Matthew. But it does not matter how badly you do. Just give it a go. That's all we ask.' Matthew interpreted this to mean that only his *very best* was good enough. He has a pathological fear of making mistakes at the best of times. So, given his enhanced stress levels around exam time, the best intentions of his family and teachers had the completely opposite effect to what we intended.

I was further reminded of the difficulties that can arise from taking things literally by a young man with autism that I taught. He ascribed precise meanings to words. Yes meant Yes to him. It was affirmative. He had no idea of the interrogative, 'Yes?' Every day, in order to achieve his reward, he had to stay in the class group for circle time and then ask if he could go and collect his reward. How many times did he come to me and say, 'Mr Stanton?' I would reply, 'Yes?' and he would take that as an affirmative and go off to get his reward without asking, 'Is it time for stamps?' I had to teach myself to say, 'What do you want?' instead of the ambiguous, 'Yes?'

Being pedantic

Closely bound up with a literal approach to language is a sometimes desperate need to know. They expect there to be a definite correlation between words and ideas, for real life to aspire to the precision of a science.

Thus, Matthew has in the past been very worried by the difference between village, town and city. How are they defined? When does a large village become a small town? What are the boundaries defining a hill and a mountain? If he cannot resolve questions like these he rapidly becomes quite disillusioned with the entire subject.

Matthew has learned to tolerate some of the ambiguities and illogicalities of English, his native language. But he is totally phased by gender in French and got into a terrible state because there was no logical rule he could apply to it. As a result he has set himself against ever learning a foreign language.

Alternatives

So repetition is rarely useful and often makes matters worse, rather like shouting at a foreigner who does not understand English when you should be translating. Fortunately there are alternatives. Text is permanent and can be pondered over. Matthew, in common with many other young people with autism almost learned to read before he could speak. This proves a boon to speech therapists who have found that being able to read helps to eliminate problems such as pronoun reversal. Writing down work assignments, instructions and messages for home can ease confusion. Verbal misunderstandings are one of the most common sources of stress and friction in relation to people with autism.

This also helps to explain the popularity of the Internet as a medium for communication. Web cameras and video conferencing are not yet widely available and text based communications, either by e-mail or in real time in chat rooms remain the most common means of person to person communication over the Internet. This has a number of advantages for the person with autism.

- There are no confusing signals to misinterpret like body language, facial expression and tone of voice.

- They can work out their responses and edit them before they send – no more verbal gaffes!

- It is safe. If the conversation gets too much they can escape easily.

- Emoticons (**Emot**ional **icons**) give unambiguous messages like :-) for happy or :-(meaning unhappy.

Emoticons are close relations of the rebus symbols that have been used to introduce literacy skills to many learning disabled children and augment communication in children who find verbal interaction difficult (Detheridge 1998).

Instead of adding to the verbal overload, symbols can give clear and unambiguous signals to youngsters and adults that remain when the spoken words are just confused echoes. More important, they provide a direct approach to communication by the person with autism.

They can be used in conjunction with schemes such as the Picture Exchange Communication System where the physical transfer of the symbol from one person to another also makes explicit the notion of communication as a transaction between people instead of an action by one person.

The importance of communication as a social interaction rather than an individual skill was brought home to me by a young man who used signing to communicate his needs but had no idea that communication was a two way process. He sometimes signed with his back to you so you could not see the sign. Then he became angry and confused when people did not respond and meet his needs. Another, more able youngster expressed a similar difficulty when he complained that he had learned to speak before he learned how to communicate.

CHAPTER 14

Difficulties at School

The need for partnership

One of the impediments to providing an appropriate education for our children is the lack of trained staff who understand autism. We parents set out to educate the schools ourselves because, by and large, their experience and understanding of autism is so limited that they just do not understand our children.

This can be difficult. Schools take a pride in their professional expertise. They are supposed to know best. As a teacher I have been there myself. I am the 'expert' who is going to deliver the solution. I may welcome parents as assistants, while seeing the child's problems as a challenge for me to overcome. Even when parents are acknowledged as partners it is easy to forget our children's own insights and expertise.

In part this is a consequence of the career structure within teaching which is hierarchical and takes the most skilled and experienced teachers and promotes them to management positions from where they continue to dispense wisdom and professional expertise down through the system. Staff tend to look up rather than outside the hierarchy for advice. Your head of department probably does know more about the latest curriculum developments than most parents. But it is the parents who have read a shelf of books and acquired an intimate knowledge of their own child's autism. Within the school it may be a classroom assistant or other member of the non-teaching staff who has this knowledge and insight into the child with autism. In Matthew's case it was a classroom assistant who had known him longer than anyone else in the school who was the first to ask, 'Could this be autism?' Often it is the midday supervisor who is his only refuge in the unstructured confusion and socially explosive mayhem of the lunch break who can tell you more about his autism than the teacher who only sees the able student in a well ordered classroom.

So it is up to the school to seek out and identify all the available expertise rather than look only to the designated post holders. This sort of cultural shift is not always easy to bring about. At the very least though schools should be drawing on parental expertise. It may be more appropriate for parents to work with schools where their children are not pupils. Within my own local branch of the National Autistic Society (NAS) I can think of a few parents who are quite capable of leading in-service training courses on autism. It is probably better on balance if their talents are used in schools where they do not have to declare an interest. But they are an under-used fund of skills and knowledge at present.

The difficulties schools face

The current pressures on schools also militate against autism friendly policies. They often feel that they are being judged on a narrow academic basis in a competitive environment. They find it hard to understand that straight A pupils need the social skills curriculum even at the expense of academic subjects. Sometimes they question the need for speech and language therapy because of our children's apparently mature use of language. They do not appreciate that our children have talked like that since they were three or four while their social understanding of language may also have remained at the pre-school level. At one point Matthew almost stopped relating to boys his own age and I have watched him bamboozled by the social skills of the eight year old down the street. The effort that is needed to accommodate someone with autism: curriculum modification; adapting the learning environment that already suits the majority to fit the needs of our children – often on an inadequate budget – makes demands on staff time and goodwill that they may find impossible to sustain. Government and local education authorities need to be told that the true cost borne by schools of supporting our children is far in excess of their special needs allowances and comparable to the cost incurred with placements at specialist autistic schools. Without the unpaid hours put in by teachers and classroom assistants the system would probably collapse. And all the good will in the world cannot compensate for the lack of understanding and adverse pressures that lead many to quit school for home education or to drop out completely.

Remedial versus prosthetic models of support

Even the special needs culture in mainstream schools is not always amenable to children with autism. Traditionally special needs have been met in mainstream schools using a remedial model: identify the problem, correct it and move on. You put the support in, the kid does well, you take the support away. OK for a temporary difficulty but for people with autism this is the equivalent of teaching someone to walk on crutches and when they can do it you take the crutch away and wonder why they fall down! Support for our children is prosthetic. It is a long term commitment, not a short term fix. The crutch may be exchanged for a walking stick, disguised as an umbrella or spend most of its time in the stand by the door. But it always has to be there for the times when it is needed.

Special needs departments used to be known as remedial classes in the UK. The move towards integration and inclusion for all pupils has meant that this model and the schools themselves have had to be adapted, especially in the realm of physical and sensory impairment. But in the sphere of learning difficulties there is still a tendency to regard pupil problems as obstacles to be overcome by the expertise of the special needs department. If a child presents with apparently intractable problems that do not respond to short term 'fixes' then the efficacy of the placement is questioned and specialist provision elsewhere is suggested.

The remedial model together with the resistance to labelling can have serious consequences for the child with autism. They are often too bright for the curriculum available to their autistic peers in special school but too socially naive to get by within mainstream. They do not fit either model. If they are to be maintained within a mainstream setting that offers a curriculum to match their intellectual ability, then the schools as well as the parents need clear signposts that will lead them to understand and cater for the special needs that arise from our children's autism.

Study skills

It is also no surprise that many people with autism do very well at school. They spend a great deal of time and use a great deal of intelligence studying people around them in order to fathom the mysteries of social existence. Compared to the study of humanity, mathematics or science often appeal for their logic and predictability.

What schools often find hard to understand is how quite able young people with autism can struggle academically. This is because autistic intelligence, like every other aspect of the disorder, can offer quite penetrating skills and abilities. But the consequences can be quite devastating for other spheres of activity.

Temple Grandin is well known as a person with autism who has written extensively about the condition. She is a powerful visual thinker and describes her mind thus, 'My mind is like a CD-ROM in a computer, like a quick-access videotape. But once I get there I have to play the whole part' (Sacks 1995).

In this way she designs cattle handling facilities for farms, stockyards and slaughterhouses down to the last detail in her head before committing them to paper. Once the design is complete it is fixed in her mind and transferring it to paper is a purely mechanical act.

However she has great difficulty with abstract thought and has to translate even a quite simple proverb like 'a rolling stone gathers no moss' into visual imagery before she can give it meaning. According to Sacks, 'She has to concretize before she can generalize.'

Matthew had great difficulty with the fact that I was an atheist and his teachers were Christian. We were adults and we disagreed! Whatever happened to truth? Eventually he accepted that some truths were matters of fact and others were matters of belief but still cannot assign knowledge to these categories by himself. Although he likes history he is better with narratives than comparing rival interpretations or questioning the motives of historical characters.

Problems with writing

Like Temple Grandin, Matthew has no trouble with working things out in his head. He also uses computer imagery to describe the process. But once the work is done transcription is not the painless process for him that it is for her. He dictated this account of his writing problems to me.

I have real problems putting ideas down on paper or on an LCD screen. I have thoughts but there is too much time and work with my fingers holding the pen and writing or typing so that my ideas get muddled, lost and just go. I got these thoughts and I'm writing them down but there is so much work and not enough time to write them down. Work = turning thoughts into sentences to put down on the page and the physical act of writing or typing. You have to write it in a certain specific order before the thought can become realized on the page or the screen.

I could speak each thought to myself in my mind, arrange the text on the screen in my brain. But then it takes so long to write it down and put in all the speech marks, full stops commas and punctuation and spelling and I have to think about forming every letter. That is why I am a slow writer and cannot write much.

Sometimes I spend a long time getting all the ideas or the story worked out on the screen in my brain and then I do not have enough time to write it down. In the end writing is only there to let the teacher see what is in your mind. It does not matter how it gets down on the paper. Ink and paper is one way and it is not very easy to correct the mistake. When you are speaking it is very easy and quick to correct the mistake.

Bullying

A school may be justly proud of its anti bullying policy and caring ethos. Yet when faced with a claim of systematic bullying the school goes onto the defensive, demanding proof, challenging the young person's version of events. Under pressure the pupil with autism will admit that nobody actually hit him. It was just some silly name calling.

But this name calling can be just as hurtful and threatening as actual violence. Racial abuse of minorities is quite rightly viewed as anathema by education authorities. Schools operate zero tolerance when physical or sensory handicaps are the subject of ridicule and taunts. But the lad with autism is supposed to laugh off the whispered taunts: 'Schizo', 'Mental'. Girls make sexual advances. If he responds he is cruelly rebuffed. If he ignores them he is accused of being gay.

Cumine, Leach and Stevenson (1998) use a case study in which a boy with autism brings a screwdriver to school to protect himself from bullies. There is no evidence of bullying and he is threatened with exclusion until a specialist teacher observes low level teasing and bullying in unsupervised situations like the corridors and playground. It is easy to see how a child with autism who lacks the ability to shrug this off or deflect it with humour reacts angrily. The other children are shocked by his response which increases his isolation and what may have begun as gentle teasing escalates into bullying the 'weirdo'. He responds in kind until we reach the totally inappropriate and dangerous response that would normally lead to exclusion. When the autism is understood instead of punishment he is given additional support.

Something similar happened with my own son. We had told him that bullies are usually cowards and if you stand up to them they back down. So he did. Unfortunately he did it in the school library and proceeded to throttle his tormentor in view of a member of staff. The school has a strict policy that should have seen him excluded but waived the penalty in his case.

Children with autism sometimes imagine they are being bullied or teased when they are not. Their social impairment often leads people with autism to misread the motives of others. But if certain incidents or behaviours are perceived as bullying by them *it is that perception that counts.*

When reading posts in e-mail groups one often gets responses like, 'That could have been *my* son you were describing!' This perception of bullying seems remarkably consistent.

The single thing that sets off Matthew's anger is when he feels he is being teased. In fact the situation might not actually involve teasing, but he interprets the comments or laughter as being directed toward him.

People with autism crave certainty and will impose it in situations that do not warrant it. Shades of grey and balance of probabilities are not familiar concepts for them. If somebody says something hurtful they must have done it on purpose; otherwise why say it? Accidents do not happen. Mistakes are not to be tolerated. If *I* know that that remark is only going to make matters worse why don't *you* know? You must have known. And so you did it on purpose.

It is just as likely that the person with autism will be put at risk by their social naiveté. Because the bully tells them he wants to be their friend they believe him and, because the code says you do not tell on friends the tormentor is given carte blanche. The really lonely child is often so desperate for friends that they accept a degree of rough treatment as the price of acceptance. They become the group fall guy or stooge, a butt for cruel jokes. In exchange their idiosyncrasies *may* be tolerated or even encouraged for their entertainment value and protection given against rival groups.

I use the word '*may*' advisedly. When the group eventually tires of him, the child with autism may not understand that he is being rejected. His social naiveté is no longer a source of amusement but of annoyance. They want rid of him but he keeps going back for more because they are his friends. They must be. They said so. Either they are lying now or they were lying then and people do not lie about friendship It is too important. So why are they so cruel to him now?

Too clever by half?

A big problem with Asperger syndrome is that because the subject can demonstrate an intelligent grasp of his or her problems and talk intelligently about them the school expects that same intellectual ability to lead to a solution. Believe me, if logic and argument were sufficient to talk someone out of their autism, Matthew would be cured by now! One of the biggest mental leaps that the neuro-typical have to make and the greatest test of our theory of mind is whether we can put ourselves in the mind of a person with autism and imagine what it must be like to have a complete handle on the problem while being unable to comprehend or accept the solution.

An American adult with autism suggested to me that if school officials have difficulty comprehending how a youngster can understand his problem so well but have no clue as to the solution, I should try this analogy with them.

A physics student does his doctoral thesis on baseball pitches. He carefully analyses exactly what causes curve balls, sliders, and knuckle balls to move. Now, ask those school officials if they think that physics student would make a great major-league baseball pitcher. In fact, would he even be able to pitch effectively in the lowest level of the minor leagues? Just as understanding the scientific principles behind various pitches does not make a man a great pitcher, or even a fairly good one, understanding one's own social limitations does not enable one to overcome those limitations. You do not need to understand baseball to get this point. But it might help you to understand autism.

We had an illustration of this with Matthew's obsessive compulsive disorder (OCD). This affects maybe five million people in the USA and one million in the UK (Rapaport 1994) making it more prevalent than autism. Many children with autism are also prone to OCD. Matthew's obsession is with hygiene and he is a compulsive hand washer.

Recently he decided that he had heard all the arguments and really, after washing your hands in the bathroom it was not necessary to wash them again in the kitchen sink. So, without telling us, he waited until he was on holiday, in a relaxed situation. He knows that increased stress just exacerbates his compulsions. He washed his hands before eating then sat in the kitchen and ate with his fingers, making sure he put his fingers in his mouth to prove to himself that he was satisfied with their cleanliness.

When he went to put his plate in the sink he still had to wash his hands. He could not understand this. These fingers had been in his mouth! He knew they were clean. Yet, still he had to wash them. He said it felt like instinct. When he explained this to his psychiatrist he rationalized it thus. He had listened to all the arguments. He accepted the arguments. He wanted to stop and he had stopped. Yet he still had to wash when he went to the sink. His medication was supposed to help with obsessions. He had kept to his side of the deal. The medication must have failed. Because this was the only explanation that seemed to make sense it had to be true. When first the psychiatrist and then I begged to differ we had a period of meltdown. It was only much later that day that he was able to accept that 'it is not by will alone'. Not even willpower allied to courage, intelligence and medication was enough to conquer his obsession. He needs an additional programme of help from a trained therapist. Luckily, the local health service psychology department is able to provide that.

People with autism often make excessive demands on themselves. Perfectionism brings its own pressures: like the boy who spent a month designing the perfect title page for his project but did not do any work on the content. One of the reasons Matthew had such a stressful reaction to exams was his mistaken belief that you had to get 100%. We thought we were winning when he accepted that his personal, attainable best and not the absolute best was the target. But we were unprepared for his negative reaction to an 85% score in a science test when he had decided that 95% was his 'attainable best'.

CHAPTER 15

The Way Forward

Recipe for success

I do not have the solution to the question of how to meet the educational needs of young people with autism. Nobody does. But here are some essential ingredients. Awareness and understanding of autism has to increase. The experience of people with autism and their parents has to be heeded. The best practise from the specialist educators and therapists needs to be widely shared. Schools must have the support to experiment and implement new ideas. Above all we have to heed this timely reminder from an adult with autism.

*I realise that you parents want your children to be able to function in normal society, but so long as we are **happy**, do not hurt anyone else, are able to make a living for ourselves, why force us into your niche? (And yes, I do realise that some people **do** have destructive tendencies that need to be taken care of) I have learned over the years what to do to function in society. (If I hit someone, I may get thrown in jail. If I am rude to people, no one will want to talk to me, etc.) In my humble opinion, you parents **should** 'smooth the edges' enough so that we can function in society, but to try to make your children be **exactly** like an 'average' child is a mistake.*

Integration and inclusion – the least restrictive environment

Integration or segregation? Inclusion or exclusion? The buzz words may have changed over the years but the value judgement implicit in the language is the same. And, for the most part, parents and children with high functioning autism do want inclusion. The problems arise when inclusion breaks down. If the policy of inclusion is poorly implemented or the child has needs that the mainstream school are unable to meet there have to be alternatives. Otherwise inclusion actually comes to mean exclusion for the children who spend months and sometimes years as non-attenders while parents and education officers argue over what is to be done.

The concept of the least restrictive environment is a legal entitlement in the USA. This takes us out of the false dichotomy of 'inclusion good, exclusion bad'. All social environments are restrictive of the individual in some way. All schools impose restrictions on their pupils. Sometimes the person with autism cannot handle normal peer group pressure and school stresses them out completely. Then they need support to overcome this difficulty.

It is the unwelcome restrictions that we find most difficult to countenance. When our autistic children are bullied and teased by peers who have no awareness or understanding of autism this is not 'the least restrictive environment'. When educators and other professionals think that our kids are the problem because they cannot handle the bullying these professionals are not providing 'the least restrictive environment'. When governments set targets for exam results and impose penalties for failure they are further restricting the environment for all pupils. They make it more difficult for schools to take a flexible approach to the range of special needs including autism.

We are also extremely suspicious of attempts to promote inclusion as a zero cost option, financed by the closure of all those 'bad,' exclusive special schools and units. If inclusion is such a good thing that we would have to be mad to refuse it why not put the money and thought into it and show that you know how to make it work properly? Then you can transfer the skills and resources from your special schools into the all-singing all-dancing inclusive education system and none of us will mind.

There is still a long way to go. It is clearly a nonsense to provide wheelchair access on every floor and forget about the stairs. But this is analogous to the levels of autism awareness we sometimes meet. Just as schools have carried out significant structural alterations to accomodate pupils with physical handicaps, so they need support from the policy makers for the equally radical changes to school culture that are needed if they are to welcome our pupils. Meanwhile, if a special school is more conducive to positive learning outcomes and enhanced self-esteem parents will continue to pursue that choice.

But in making that choice the more academically able pupil with autism has fewer options in this respect than his autistic cousins further along the spectrum. There is very little provision for able pupils who cannot manage mainstream schooling. In the UK special needs departments operate to support pupils within inclusive classes. There may be withdrawal for specific lessons or support work but pupils who are academically able are expected to cope with the National Curriculum. If they have psychological or emotional problems that prevent this there is a system of pupil referral units that is not really suited to children with autism, who have enough problems dealing with normal social interaction without having to cope with a restricted peer group that is largely emotionally and behaviourally disturbed.

In the USA there are resource classes, which are self-contained classes within mainstream schools for pupils whose need for special help outweighs their entitlement to full integration. These too are not always a suitable option for the child with autism. Time and again parents report that the teachers think their child with high functioning autism would get more help in a resource class. Sometimes this is true but often they have to choose between this and the social contact their child needs in the mainstream. They may become isolated and bored in a special resource class and need the stimulation of their NT peers.

There are specialist schools for children with Asperger syndrome. But they are expensive and few and far between. There will always be a place for them within the range of provision but most young people with high functioning autism will continue to find themselves within the mainstream for educational provision.

Getting it right

Success stories like the following are easier to come by in the primary and middle schools than in the secondary sector. But this account holds lessons for us all.

> *Hi, I have a 13 year old daughter with ADD and Asperger's who is just completing her 8th year in French Immersion in Canada. (Our family is English speaking otherwise.) Her success is largely due to:*

- *Funding: the half time teachers' aid (some trained in how to deal with children like herself, others who were just warm bodies, and one who was a good demonstration to her on how not to act in public. Everyone has their own lesson to teach.)*

- *Constant awareness as to how she was doing by the teacher, administration (vice-principal), school board person in charge of grants, resource person, her parents, and anyone else who cared by verbal and written reports. We go into her locker and back pack all the time looking for assignments and completed work. She will finish projects and forget to hand them in. Of course you hear more when they are doing badly. When she is co-operating, they all move onto other children.*

- *Friendship circle (when she was in grade 1, her classmates took turns being her friend for the day or week depending on their enthusiasm. By grade 3 she had managed to get it together for the social skills to have a best friend, instead of tagging along in a group. She has always had friends in higher and lower grades. She changed best friends every year, but this year's model has been her best friend three times now. Gentle correction on the spot by a peer was the key here to teach friendship social skills.*

She has always responded well to medication. She takes a com-
bination of Ritalin and Tegretol. She is 5 foot 4 inches tall and
weighs 150 lb. This has not affected her growth. We (her) parents
were at school a lot. They stay for lunch there, so we took her out
once a week when she was younger, less now. I volunteer in the
library once a week. It's a good job and I enjoy it. I will also
volunteer in the high school library next year. We helped in the
classroom, we went on school trips, we joined the parent council,
we were present.

We also have other children. Sometimes we would be in their
classrooms, but she knew we were around. This helped greatly in
convincing her not to impulsively be rude to teachers. You cannot
learn if you are always out in the hall being punished.

These are just some to the things that we do. Next year she goes into
High School (grade nine to 12) here. Its a different school with a
different set of expectations. Wish us luck.

Friendship circles and buddy systems

The previous reference to a 'friendship circle' is very important.
Sometimes the most important support we can give our children
carries no resource implications at all. Peer group pressure may
be devastating for our kids but peer group support can be a real
life saver. Teachers naturally shy away from focusing on handicaps and disabilities and try to avoid labelling kids. But the child
in a wheelchair has no way of hiding their disability and because
it is so obvious it has to be dealt with in the open.

Once we get a diagnosis we have to be up front about our
children's problems and educate their school mates from the
early years onwards about autism. We are not shielding our kids
when we avoid public labelling. Eventually their otherness
becomes apparent to the other children who provide their own
labels: schizo; psycho; gay boy. (A lot of teenage male culture is

very homophobic and our children's social and sexual naiveté is open to misinterpretation.)

So early diagnosis, peer group awareness and acceptance leading to a buddy system in which the kids understand and protect their autistic friends, can provide support throughout a child's education. A good example of this came from a mother in my local NAS branch. She described how the head teacher at her son's junior school was trying to explain autism to his year group. Many of them had grown up with him, supported him through infant school and knew all about his problems. Their reaction was, 'Why is she picking on him just because he is autistic? He's our mate!'

Transition to secondary school

Primary schools are more autism friendly than secondary schools. They are usually smaller. The curriculum and timetable are less rigidly confined by the pressures of the public examination system. You spend most of the year with the same teacher in the same room for all your lessons. Perhaps most important of all you do not have to socialize with teenage boys.

The problem is, how do we combine structure and security for the student and a flexible response to their problems in the atmosphere of a typical secondary school, constrained by the needs of maybe 1000+ students? It is as if our children have grown up in the company of and acquired the attitude of mind of artisans from a rural workshop. They are then expected to cope with the equivalent of urban factory conditions in a manner analogous to the social upheaval and distress that so exercised our forebears during the Industrial Revolution. And this for people with an inherent resistance to change!

Diversity and choice

Education has come a long way from the days when there was one set of questions and only one answer to every question. Nowadays, school students are invited to discuss, to empathize, to compare and weigh up the evidence and decide. The pupil with autism soon acquires a quite acute awareness of how easy it is to be wrong on a whole range of issues and may prefer to be told the answer rather than be exposed to further ridicule and shame by risking an opinion. Thus, much of modern pedagogy, while quite admirable in its intentions is less than user friendly to the student with autism.

With this in mind it was interesting to receive a letter from a man educated as a white South African during the apartheid regime. Teaching was very didactic – no child centred education there! Structure and discipline were quite rigid. An honour code among students protected the weak from bullying. This man, with autism, thrived and prospered in this environment. For a liberal-minded egalitarian like myself it is ironic that the anathema of apartheid should have seemingly thrown up an ideal environment for the education of at least one child with autism.

I am not arguing for a return to traditional values or rolling back the educational reforms of the last 50 years. Rather, we have to recognize that diversity and choice are essential elements if we are to meet the needs of all pupils in an inclusive education system. If mainstream schools are enabled to adapt and take on board the successful ideas developed in specialist educational settings those elements of diversity and choice can be extended to include the special needs of children with autism.

Apart from training to develop autism awareness and understanding of the principles behind successful methods of intervention such as TEACCH and SPELL the most important resource schools need is time. More and more the schools are driven by external events such as the cycle of inspection, national testing, league tables and the reporting of exam results. High scoring schools are widely regarded as good schools and they probably are. Bad schools tend not to get favourable reports or good exam results. But this competitive ethos seems to run counter to the comprehensive principle of equal opportunity for all. How much time should a school spend on developing social skills in a pupil with autism, especially if it is a learning outcome that is not easily measured or celebrated by test results? Would the time be better spent on a small group of borderline pupils who could make a difference to the school reaching its literacy targets?

If other, less tangible targets could be equally valued and the range of measures of a good school broadened to include them it would make a difference. But the schools still need the time to meet all these needs. The only way to buy time in a school is to pay for additional teaching staff. And the only way schools will pay for this time is if they are properly funded and given a clear indication that this use of the additional time is supported by government agencies and will be given positive reinforcement.

Flexi-schooling

Part of the problem for our children is that schools as organizations need to function in certain ways if they are to operate effectively and deliver the curriculum that is expected of them. Unfortunately, this can create problems for our children. They need routines that are tailor made to suit their needs. Mainstream secondary schools cannot always respond with this degree of flexibility.

In this case we may have to develop our own system of flexi-schooling. Many of our young people would do better in a campus situation – selecting from the curriculum options on offer plus additional support for social skills, speech and language etc.

One way this could work is via home schooling. Only instead of working at home and seeing your home school tutor one day a week we could set up a home schooling centre, a house in a residential area where a group of secondary age kids with autism meet to do their home schooling. By pooling their special needs allowances the parents in partnership with the LEA or local school board could combine to buy equipment and hire a specialist teacher. The children could stay on the roll of their neighbourhood school and have access to resources such as the library and visit the school part time for certain lessons.

Therapists and clinicians could visit the home-school-house and find all their clients in one place for cognitive behavioural therapy, the social skills curriculum, speech and language, music therapy etc. If Johnny is mad about dinosaurs he can explore the web and develop IT skills around his hobby there. Physical Education? Arrange trips to local health clubs and swimming pools if school PE lessons are too traumatic. For science use the kitchen and the garden as laboratories. If you need more advanced facilities then local schools and colleges could be approached.

Often teenagers with autism do better in the company of adults doing a night school course than they would with their peers. Everyone else wants to be in the class. They have chosen to learn and often paid for the privilege. It is easier to find a sympathetic adult to mentor the youngster with autism on a course like that, which often leads to an accredited qualification or exam credit.

The home school house would not be a school. Instead it would become a resource centre for all local people with autism. It would stay open at weekends and in the school holidays. Clubs and self help groups could use it as a base in the evenings.

It would be the Education Authority's job to fund such a scheme in partnership with health and welfare agencies as well as to monitor it and ensure that education was broad, balanced and relevant. I think it would be better than the enforced absence of so many due to stress. In these circumstances parents sometime opt to home educate. But this often signals the end of

LEA involvement rather than the commencement of a more fruitful partnership.

The range of available interventions

When it come to choosing how to intervene there are many autism-specific educational approaches such as Applied Behaviour Analysis which is very intensive and objective oriented, The Options Approach, which is equally intensive but totally child centred, Daily Life Therapy which emphasizes group work, music and rhythmic exercise and TEACCH, with its emphasis on the structure of the learning environment. Along with the National Autistic Society's SPELL and Early Bird approaches in the UK, all recognize the pervasive nature of autism.

While every approach has its advocates and its critics they all have more in common than they may care to acknowledge and all have demonstrated their effectiveness. See for example the paper by Fiona Knott (1995) which offers an interesting survey of approaches to autism in the USA and compares them with the UK approach as practised by the NAS.

The TEACCH approach is adaptable to a mainstream setting. It aims to support the person with autism in their environment. So you compensate for the pupil's autism by altering the environment and making it autism friendly. The main points are:

- a schedule or structure to the day that is predictable and easily communicable to the individual

- clear expectations of what is expected to complete individual work assignments

- an adapted environment to remove sensory distractions

- an understanding that unstructured 'fun time' and the organized chaos of some group activities is hard work for our children and they need additional support at these times.

TEACCH seminars are regularly held in the UK. They have a comprehensive web site and if you live in the USA you can visit Division TEACCH at the University of North Carolina from where it has grown to encompass a state wide cradle to the grave service model for all people with autism.

The SPELL approach is used in NAS schools in the UK and has much to recommend it. SPELL is an acronym for:

Structured environment

Positive approach to the person with autism

Empathy with their point of view

Low arousal, intervening calmly and being non-confrontational

Links with parents and the wider community.

The SPELL approach is less a method and more about our attitude to people with autism. While schools in the USA will adhere to TEACCH or ABA or one of the other methods exclusively, NAS schools are likely to be more eclectic and adopt a pick and mix approach, incorporating elements of TEACCH structure, behavioural programmes and child centred play based activities in programmes tailored to the individual needs of children.

It is tempting for local health and education authorities to opt for 'a one size fits all' solution, a single package that combines administrative and financial convenience. Unfortunately all children are congenitally inconvenient and children with autism are refreshingly normal in this respect. What works for your child might not work for mine and provision, ideally, should be based on the child's individual profile and not their geographical profile. Realistically, if an area has a centre of excellence offering one kind of intervention they are going to go with that. Parents expect this but would certainly welcome diversity and a willingness to send their child across the financial boundary to another authority's provision, if this was more suitable in their particular case. Meanwhile, it is lack of expertise rather than inappropriate expertise that bedevils most of us. And all of the available resources for children with autism are hopelessly oversubscribed.

The whole point is to be flexible in our planning approach and develop initiatives out of local opportunities while remaining consistent in our adherence to principles of respect for and understanding of people with autism.

CHAPTER 16

Conclusion

This book grew out of the therapeutic advice of my stress counsellor to write down my anger and deal with it before moving on. Much of this stemmed from my concerns for my son. It seems appropriate that as I approach the end of the book the outlook for Matthew is more positive than at any time in the last six years.

We had wanted the school to change dramatically to meet his individual needs as a person with autism. The school felt confident that they could meet his normal academic needs within the mainstream curriculum but felt unqualified for the task we had in mind. So it was all or nothing.

Now we no longer expect the earth from our education authority. Though, God knows, we still think he deserves it! They in turn no longer expect Matthew to conform to the norm. He attends school part time. They pay for externally provided placements involving life skills and work experience along with outward bound type challenges. There are still major gaps in his education but these are being addressed. This flexibility means that we can incorporate a therapeutic regime for his OCD. Overall this suits him. He is back in a routine, no longer housebound by fear, and his mental health is as good as it has ever been. He has stopped down a year to avoid the hectic pace and inflexibility of the exam driven timetable that dominates the final two years of the English secondary syllabus.

We do not know what will happen next year. We understand that without resources that at present do not exist the school will not, in all conscience be able to combine a flexible timetable for Matthew with the rigorous needs of his peers on the examination timetable. We may have to make other arrangements in partnership with our LEA. At least we feel we have a partnership now.

There are two photographs of Matthew that seem to mark the path that he is following. One is a press photo of the crowd at a football match. It is a cup tie and our team has just scored the winning goal in injury time. The whole crowd rise from their seats to salute our victory, all that is except Matthew. His is the only face in the picture turned away from the pitch as he asks me what is happening. Two years later I have a picture of him at Plymouth Hoe, part of a crowd of 45000 people assembled to witness the eclipse. His face is glowing. He is happy. He belongs. He understands what is happening and feels a part of it.

When well meaning adults tell him he will grow out of his autism as he gets older he tells them, 'No. I will always be autistic. I need help to grow into it, not out of it.'

References

Abell, F., Ashburner, J., Frackowiack, R., Friston, Frith, C., Frith, U.K., Happé, F., Krams, M. and Passingham, R. (1999) 'The neuroanatomy of autism: A voxel based whole brain analysis of structural scans.' *NeuroReport 10*, 1647–1651
available on http://www.neurosite.com/

Artingstall, K. A. (1995) *Munchausen's Syndrome by Proxy.* FBI Law Enforcement Bulletin
available on http://www.lectlaw.com/files/cri15.htm

Asperger, H. Die 'Autistischen Psychopathie' im Kindersalter. (Translated by U. Frith in Frith (1991) below.)

Attwood, T. (1998) *Asperger's Syndrome: A Guide for Parents and Professionals.* London: Jessica Kingsley Publishers

Attwood, T. (1999) *Asperger's Syndrome: Diagnosis and Support.* (video) London: Jessica Kingsley Publishers

Baron-Cohen, S. and Bolton, P. (1993) *Autism: The Facts.* Oxford: Oxford University Press

Channel 4 (1992) *A is for Autism.* Available from the National Autistic Society

Connor, M.J. (1999) 'Children with autism as victims of abuse.' *Autism: CURRENT ISSUES 9*
available on http://www.jaymuggs.demon.co.uk/connor6.htm

Cumine, V., Leach, J. and Stevenson, G. (1998) *Asperger Syndrome: A Practical Guide for Teachers.* London: David Fulton Publishers

Debbaudt, D. (1999) *Avoiding Unfortunate Situations.*
http://homepages.infoseek.com/~ddpi/ddpi.html

Dekker, M.(1999) *ON OUR OWN TERMS: Emerging Autistic Culture.* Autism 99 on-line Conference
available on http://www.autism99.org/html/Papers/html/

Department of Education and Science (1978) *Special Educational Needs; the Report of the Committee of Enquiry into the Education of Handicapped children and Young People (Chairman; Mrs. M. Warnock)* Cmnd 7212. London: HMSO

Detheridge, T.and Detheridge, M. (1997) *Literacy Through Symbols; Improving Access for Children and Adults.* London: David Fulton Publishers

Donaldson, M. (1978) *Children's Minds.* London: Fontana/Collins

Evans, G. (1999) *Group Work with Siblings of Children with Autism.* Autism 99 on-line Conference available on **http://www.autism99.org/html/Papers/html/**

Frith, U. (1989) *Autism, Explaining the Enigma.* Oxford: Basil Blackwell

Frith, U. (ed) (1991) *Autism and Asperger Syndrome.* Cambridge: Cambridge University Press

Gould J. (1998) 'Labelling parents; a substitute for diagnosing children? Munchausen's syndrome by proxy.' *Communication* Winter 1998, 25–26.

Greenspan, S.I., Weider, S. and Simon, R. (1998) *The Child with Special Needs: Encouraging Intellectual and Emotional Growth.* Harlow: Addison-Wesley

Kanner, L. (1943) 'Autistic disturbances of affective contact.' *Nervous Child 2,* 217–250.

Kessick, R. T. C. (1999) *Autism a la Carte.* Autism 99 on-line Conference **http://www.autism99.org/html/Papers/html/**

Knott, F. (1995) *Approaches to Autism in the USA.* Report for the Winston Churchill Travelling Fellowship. (Obtainable from the author, Fiona Knott, Clinical Child Psychologist, Rainbow House, Ayrshire Central Hospital, Irvine, KA12 8SS, Scotland, UK.)

Lovaas, I.O. (1980) *Teaching Developmentally Disabled Children; the ME Book.* Austin, Texas: Pro-Ed Books

The National Autistic Society (1997) *Approaches to Autism.* London: National Autistic Society

Network News (1999) 'Hanen and autism'. *Communication* Winter 1998, 10.

Nind, M. and Hewett, D. (1996) *Access to Communication; Developing the basics of communication with people with severe learning difficulties through Intensive interaction.* London: David Fulton Publishers

Rapaport, J. (1994) *The Boy Who Couldn't Stop Washing. The Experience and Treatment of OBSESSIVE COMPULSIVE DISORDER.* London: Harper Collins Publishers

Sacks, O. (1995) *An Anthropologist on Mars.* London: Picador/ MacMillan

Segar, M. (1997) *Coping – A Survival Guide for People with Asperger Syndrome.* Early Years Diagnostic Centre, Nottingham

Shattock, P.(1999) *Environmental Factors in the Causation of Autism.* Autism 99 on-line Conference **available on http://www.autism99.org/html/Papers/html/**

Trevarthen, C., Aitken, K., Papoudi, D. and Robarts, J. (1999) *Children with Autism; Diagnosis and Intervention to Meet Their Needs 2nd edition.* London: Jessica Kingsley Publishers

Vygotsky, L. (1962) *Thought and Language.* Cambridge, MA: MIT Press

Willey, L.H. (1999) *Pretending to be Normal: Living with Asperger's Syndrome.* London: Jessica Kingsley Publishers.

Wing, L. (1998) *The Autistic Spectrum: A Guide for Parents and Professionals.* London: Constable

Resources and Organizations

The National Autistic Society
393 City Road,
London EC1V 1NG
phone 020 7833 2299
fax 020 7833 9666
email nas@nas.org.uk
web site http://www.oneworld.org/Autism_uk/

The NAS should be your first stop for information on the Early Bird Project, CHAT, SPELL and training in the use of diagnostic and assessment tools in the UK. Their website contains full details of these initiatives, an extensive list of publications and resources and links to many of the major autism related Web sites and overseas organizations and societies.

They and their affiliated organizations also maintain schools and adult services as well as providing support for individual families via help lines and nationally co-ordinates volunteers in parent to parent and befriending schemes

CHAT
Sally Wheelwright
Department of Experimental Psychology
Downing Street
Cambridge, CB2 3EB, UK
Tel: 01223 333550
Fax: 01223 333564
Email: sjw18@hermes.cam.ac.uk
http://www.oneworld.org/autism_uk/profess/chat.html

NAS EarlyBird Programme
Manager: Jane Shields
NAS EarlyBird Centre
Manvers House
Pioneer Close
Wath-Upon-Dearne
Rotherham
South Yorkshire S63 7JZ
Tel: +44 (0)1709 761273
Fax: +44 (0)1709 763234
Email: earlybird@dial.pipex.com
http://www.oneworld.org/autism_uk/nas/earlybi.html

ABA / Lovaas
Professor Lovaas can be contacted at
Psychology Department
University of California
Los Angeles
405 Hilgard Avenue
Los Angeles
California 90024–1563

In the UK contact

PEACH (Parents for Early intervention in Autistic CHildren)
PO Box 10836
London SW14 9ZN

Hanen Centre
Suite 403 – 1075 Bay Street
Toronto ON M5S 2B1
CANADA
tel: (416) 921–1073
fax: (416) 921–1225
e-mail: info@hanen.org
web site: www.hanen.org

Higashi / Daily Life Therapy
Boston Higashi School
800 North Main Street
Randolph
Massachusetts 02368

Options / SonRise Program
The Options Institute and Fellowship
2080 Undermountain Road
Sheffield
Massachusetts 01257–9718

TEACCH
Division TEACCH, Administration and Research
Medical Wing School East,
The University of North Carolina
Chapel Hill
North Carolina 27955- 4127

Resources on the World Wide Web

These are so extensive that the best method is to visit a site such as the NAS (http://www.oneworld.org/Autism_uk/) or the Autism Society of America (http://www.autism-society.org/) and follow the links from there.

In addition to the major sites that everybody links to my own particular favourites are

THE WEBSITE
(http://members.xoom.com/MagsSchwa/index.html)

created by and for people with autism and their families is a very friendly starting point for parents. It 'belongs' to members of the news groups alt.support.autism and bit.listserv.autism. These are my on line home and I thoroughly recommend them to anybody who wants to meet parents and people with autism, hear their stories and learn.

Sites by people with autism

Aeleis in Wonderland
(http://aeleis.autistics.org/)

Institute for the Study of the Neurologically Typical
(http://isnt.autistics.org/)

Greetings from Dave Spicer
(http://www.mindspring.com/~dspicer/index.html)

Thomas A. McKean's Home Pages
(http://www.geocities.com/~soonlight/)

I can also recommend the following e-mail lists

Autinet Forum
(http://homepages.iol.ie/~wise/autinet/index.htm)

Autism UK
(http://www.autism-uk.ed.ac.uk/welcome.html#begin)

Aspergers UK
(AspergersUK-owner@onelist.com)

Asperger
(http://www.egroups.com/group/asperger/info.html)

Aut-older
(aut-older-owner@onelist.com)

My e-mail address is stanton@totalise.co.uk